Enterprise Software Selection:
How to Pinpoint the Perfect Software Solution using Multiple Information Sources

Shaun Snapp

Enterprise Software Selection: How to Pinpoint the Perfect Software Solution using Multiple Information Sources

Copyright © 2013 by SCM Focus Press

For information about this title or to order other books and/or electronic media, contact the publisher:
SCM Focus Press
PO Box 29502 #9059
Las Vegas, NV 89126-9502
http://www.scmfocus.com/scmfocuspress
(408) 657-0249

ISBN: 978-1-939731-15-9

Printed in the United States of America

Cover and Interior design by: 1106 Design

Contents

CHAPTER 1

Introduction to Software Selection

Software selection is a form of forecasting, just as any other purchase decision is a forecast of how successfully the purchased item will meet expectations. Forecasting is necessary because it is not feasible to implement each application under consideration before it is purchased to see how it works in the business. A forecast requires sampling and the participants assume that the sample they take will be representative of how the software will perform when purchased. Everything from the software vendors' explanations regarding how their software works, to the review of reports by IT analysts, to the software demonstrations, are all a form of sampling.

Software selection is much more involved than other types of purchasing decisions because software—and enterprise software in particular—is complex. The software selection decision is not based solely upon the actual application, but also upon factors such as the pre-existing relationship between the buyer and the vendors, the availability of consultants trained in the software, and how the software will interact with other software currently installed and software the buyer plans to purchase in the future.

In my experience, the way in which most software selections are performed is a poor fit with this complexity because those with the domain expertise are often left out of the selection process. The involvement of the end user of the software is also an issue. In the consumer product purchasing process, the person who is going to use the product is involved directly in the decision to buy the product. In the corporate world, this is not the case, and a small group of people, who will not use the product or service make the purchase for the many people who will. If you work for a corporation and were provided with a laptop you don't like and would never buy in a million years, this is a good example of the conflicts and inefficiencies that arise when the purchaser and the consumer are two different individuals.[1] There is simply no getting around the fact that we buy differently when we are the ones who will use the product versus when someone else is going to use the product.

---

[1] One of the more amusing stories on this topic took place when I was working as a contractor for a large well-known multinational. This company shall remain nameless, but adds sugar caffeine to water and sells it for a healthy mark-up. While I bring my own laptop when I work on projects, the clients also furnish me with a laptop so I can access their systems. Ordinarily I am given a decent if boring laptop. However, this time I was given a laptop that was eight years old. I priced the laptop on eBay and found that it had a value of $480. The memory in the computer could be purchased for $10. I was supposed to help them with their optimizer, which is an advanced computer skill set, and they have given me a $480 computer.

Software selection is the most important part of any software implementation because it is the best opportunity to match the software with the business requirements, which is the most important factor in determining the success of the project. While it would be difficult to find anyone who thinks that software selection is unimportant, the vast majority of companies do not treat the selection process scientifically. Consequently, most companies are not able to zero in on the best software to meet their needs, especially when the inherent problems due primarily to conflicts of interest in many of the organizations that serve as information sources for enterprise software are factored in.

This book explains how software selection can be improved. While enterprise software is one of the most complex products purchased by companies, good software selection is not all that complicated. For instance, when I compare the complexity of this book on software selection to other books I have written, this book was considerably easier to write. However, to obtain improved results in software selection, some rules must be followed. In short, these rules inject greater structure, better documentation, and a more scientific approach into the selection process.

Books and Other Publications on Software Selection

As with all my books I perform a comprehensive literature review before I begin writing any book. One of my favorite research quotations is from the highly respected RAND Corporation, a think tank based in sunny Santa Monica, CA—a location not far from where I grew up and where I used to walk right by with my friend when I was in high school—at that time having no idea of the historically significant institution that I used to walk by on my lost surfing weekends. This is from RAND's "Standards for High Quality Research and Analysis" publication makes the following statement regarding how its research references other work.

> *"A high-quality study cannot be done in intellectual isolation: It necessarily builds on and contributes to a body of research and analysis. The relationships between a given study and its predecessors should be rich and explicit. The study team's understanding of past research should be evident in many aspects of its work, from*

the way in which the problem is formulated and approached to the discussion of the findings and their implications. The team should take particular care to explain the ways in which its study agrees, disagrees, or otherwise differs importantly from previous studies. Failure to demonstrate an understanding of previous research lowers the perceived quality of a study, despite any other good characteristics it may possess."

This is my eleventh book, and I never thought of writing a book on software selection because I assumed (incorrectly) that the topic was documented well in existing books and articles. Not until I began performing searches on the topic did I find that this was not the case. According to Amazon, two books on this topic are, *The Software Selection Questionnaire* and *A Guide to Software Package Evaluation and Selection: The R2ISC Method*. I also found several books on how to perform software selections for specific types of software:

1. *Selecting Warehouse Software from WMS & ERP Providers—Expanded Edition: Find the Best Warehouse Module or Warehouse Management System.* This book is, of course, very specific to one type of software, and gets into great detail on the criteria that should be used to evaluate warehouse management software.

2. *Selecting and Implementing Energy Trading, Transaction and Risk Management Software—a Primer.* This is another very specific software selection book.

The above books cannot be readily applied to the selection process of other software categories. Interestingly, ERP was by far the most common category of software discussed in software selection articles and academic publications. Unfortunately, I found most of this material to be tedious. Generally speaking, material on ERP software selection does not apply to the selection of other forms of enterprise software, which employ smaller teams. In addition, a major issue in the selection of ERP software is the interplay between different departments—ERP involves at least four major departments: sales, supply chain, manufacturing and finance, and can include other departments as well. Each of these departments has vastly differing interests. The number of departments and their varied interests is less of a factor on most other software selection projects, which are more narrowly focused. However, some of the lessons of ERP software selections do apply to reporting (now known as "business intelligence" software), as all departments within a company rely upon reports in one way or another.

The books listed above are must-reads if you are selecting software in the pertinent software category. Some of the rules in these books would apply across other software categories, but I felt that an all-encompassing software selection book that could apply to all categories would be desirable.

Outside of the publications mentioned previously, there is a surprising lack of material available on the overall topic of software selection. A Google search results in the same paucity of substantial information on the topic. In fact, most of the articles I found through my Google search relate to consulting companies that sell software selection services. The articles tended to be short, cover the elementary areas of software selection, and include topics such as *The Top 7 Mistakes of Software Selection.*" If an article such as this included "Get Top Management Support" as one of its points, I know the author was really mailing it in. The majority of writing on software selection is truly lightweight in nature, and does not get into the intricacies or the interpretation of information necessary to pull off a successful software selection. The items listed in Table 4 are a good example of what I am referring to.

Table 4:   Decision Analysis Spreadsheet: Example 1

| | | | Software Alternatives | | | |
| | | | System 1 | | System 2 | |
Item	Decision Criterion	Weight	Raw	Weighted	Raw	Weighted
A	Rule-based presentation	20%	1.0	20.00%	1.0	20.00%
B	Reliable/fault tolerant	10%	1.0	10.00%	1.0	10.00%
C	Scalable	10%	1.0	10.00%	1.0	10.00%
D	Product/vendor maturity	10%	0.5	5.00%	1.0	10.00%
E	Vendor support	10%	0.5	5.00%	1.0	10.00%
F	Low total cost of ownership	10%	0.0	0.00%	1.0	10.00%
G	Extensible	10%	1.0	10.00%	1.0	10.00%
H	Single-vendor solution	5%	-0.5	-2.50%	1.0	5.00%
I	Visual rules definition/administration	15%	1.0	15.00%	0.5	7.50%
	Total	**100%**		**72.5%**		**92.50%**

Software selection tends to be discussed using the above terminology. But, this book will be much different: it will provide an analysis of the institutional incentives of the major entities that provide software information to companies, and will discuss the many shades of gray that are missing from most analyses about software selection.

I found that the books and articles on software selection are consistently Pollyannaish. They tend to describe a way of performing software selection that is far from realistic for most companies. Certainly it is necessary to make recommendations for improvement; however, recommendations should not be far out of the realm of what companies can reasonably adopt or accomplish. Just as with software design, recommendations for improvements cannot only be desirable; they must be implementable. For instance, let's say someone wrote a book about losing weight, which recommended eating a perfect diet and bicycling three hours a day, six days a week. While these recommendations would certainly work, they are simply too extreme to be followed by anyone other than a small segment of the population. Therefore, it makes more sense to highlight a pathway that a large section of the readership can actually follow.

I also searched academic publications on software selection. Here I found quite a few articles. Generally I am a big supporter of referencing previous work in any of my new works, and I have done this in most of my other books. For example in *Inventory Optimization and Multi-Echelon Planning,* I dedicated an appendix to the early research papers in the field because I thought it was important that readers understand this history. However, I did not take this approach in this current book because the majority of the articles did not resonate with me or were too "mechanical" in nature. In addition, as a group, they have a different orientation regarding software selection than what I want to present in this book. If you have read books or articles on software selection in the past, you will find this book to be completely different. Most information on software selection is about how to do things such as setting up the team, filling out the software selection questionnaire, and sending out the RFP to the vendors. These software selection topics make up only one chapter of this book. Instead, this book is focused on how to interpret the information used by the software selection team to make the decision. As there is very little information on this topic, there is little previous work to reference.

The Book's Scientific Method Orientation

I recall having a discussion with a colleague more than a decade ago, when I worked for a software vendor, about what I perceived as emotionalism on the part of our client. His viewpoint was that the software purchase and implementation had an emotional dimension because the outcome would be important to the client; therefore, it was perfectly natural to expect such emotionalism. I think he was providing some insight to how our client was behaving at the time. However, I propose that some of this emotionalism was related to the fact that the software selection that preceded the implementation had not been managed scientifically. Most material that I read as background research for this book did not really treat software selection as something that should be viewed through the lens of scientific testing. Certainly many of the articles discussed how to add structure to the process, but not how to make the overall process more scientific. This book will depart from the other available material and explain how to improve software selection along scientific lines.

My Background and the Book's Focus and Orientation

It's important to explain my background. I am an author and consultant, and spent my career in advanced supply chain planning software. My career has provided me with exposure to not only supply chain software, but also to ERP, reporting, middleware and infrastructure software. What I found working across these areas is that the lessons from one area apply consistently to the other areas. So for instance, there is a chapter in this book related to how to use and interpret the information provided by software vendors. While the specifics of the information provided by vendors differ by software category, many of the approaches tend to be the same regardless of the category. This is one of the reasons I decided to write a general book on software selection rather than a book specific to just advanced planning software. Here are a few more reasons as to why I took this approach:

1. As there are so few books on software selection, writing a book concentrated on my particular software category would mean that people focused on other software categories would not be interested in this book—which provides information that is universally applicable.

2. Creating a general book on software selection lost little. I still use some examples from the software categories in which I have experience, but these examples apply equally to any other type of enterprise software.

The one software area where this book would not apply is to the consumer software market. The consumer software market is far more efficient than the enterprise software market. In fact, I consider the consumer software market to be well supplied with information regarding software selection through magazines such as *MacWorld, PC Magazine,* or even Amazon. Resources such as these do not exist for the enterprise software space. While some of the information outlets for consumer software are biased, a very heavy bias exists in the entities that provide information about the enterprise software market, as I will explain in this book. Accounting for this bias is one of the most important factors in making a good software selection, and yet this bias is *almost undiscussed* in the literature about software selection. I read a number of publications on software selection that recommended the reader hire a consulting company to assist in their software selection, without ever explaining the incentives that affect the consulting company. I find that type of advice quite appalling. It may not be flattering to write about this topic, but if one is going to recommend a course of action, it's important that all the details are explained.

How Writing Bias Is Controlled at SCM Focus and SCM Focus Press

Bias is a serious problem in the enterprise software field. Large vendors receive uncritical coverage of their products, and large consulting companies recommend the large vendors that have the resources to hire and pay consultants rather than the vendors with the best software for the client's needs.

Just as in my consulting practice, I do not financially benefit from a company's decision to buy an application that I showcase in print, either in a book or on the website. SCM Focus has stringent rules related to controlling bias and restricting commercial influence of any information provider. These "writing rules" are provided in the link below:

http://www.scmfocus.com/writing-rules/

If other information providers followed these rules, I would be able to learn about software without being required to perform my own research and testing for every topic.

Information about enterprise supply chain planning software can be found on the Internet, but this information is primarily promotional or written at such a high level that none of the important details or limitations of the application are exposed; this is true of books as well. When only one enterprise software application is covered in a book, one will find that the application works perfectly; the application operates as expected and there are no problems during the implementation to bring the application live. This is all quite amazing and quite different from my experience of implementing enterprise software. However, it is very difficult to make a living by providing objective information about enterprise supply chain software, especially as it means being critical at some point. I once remarked to a friend that SCM Focus had very little competition in providing untarnished information on this software category, and he said, "Of course, there is no money in it."

The Approach to the Book

By writing this book, I wanted to help people get exactly the information they need without having to read a lengthy volume. The approach to the book is essentially the same as to my previous books, and in writing this book I followed the same principles.

1. **Be direct and concise.** There is very little theory in this book and the math that I cover is simple. This book is focused on software and for most users and implementers of the software the most important thing to understand is conceptually what the software is doing.

2. **Based on project experience.** Nothing in the book is hypothetical; I have worked with it or tested it on an actual project. My project experience has led to my understanding a number of things that are not covered in typical supply planning books. In this book, I pass on this understanding to you.

The SCM Focus Site

As I am also the author of the SCM Focus site, http://www.scmfocus.com, the site and the book share a number of concepts and graphics. Furthermore, this book contains many links to articles on the site, which provide more detail on specific subjects.

Intended Audience

This book has the broadest appeal of any that I have written. It should be of interest to anyone who wants to learn how to put themselves in the best possible position to make good software selection decisions about enterprise software. If you have any questions or comments about the book, please e-mail me at shaun-snapp@scmfocus.com.

Abbreviations

A listing of all abbreviations used throughout the book is provided at the end of the book.

CHAPTER 2

Understanding the Enterprise Software Market

Any selection of enterprise software happens within the context of the enterprise software market. Most people who write about the enterprise software market also work in it, and thus do not have an incentive in describing how it really works. The academic department that might be well-suited to analyzing the enterprise software market would be economists, but economists have little interest in studying how the market works. I have written some of the few articles that go so far as to analyze the enterprise software market, and these are available at the link below:

   http://www.scmfocus.com/enterprisesoftwarepolicy

In writing these articles, I have applied principles of economics, such as tests for market efficiency, anti-competitive techniques applied by certain vendors, and the industry's interaction with consulting firms and other actors. I used some of these articles in writing this book, as the nature of the enterprise software market essentially determines what is available to choose from during a software selection, and is critical to understand before making a software selection.

Background on the Enterprise Software Market

For some time it has been evident to me that the enterprise software market is not only not efficient, but is quite inefficient. Corporate customers overpay for major brands, and select software that is often not even close to the best application for their needs.

Let's cover the definition of an efficient market. An efficient market serves consumers. More often than not, customers receive good value for their purchases and don't have much of a problem finding the best product for their needs. Below I have listed important preconditions or criteria for an efficient market and, for each criterion, have analyzed the enterprise software market.

1. *Pricing is Easily Comparable:* Typically in the enterprise software market, pricing is complicated. Pricing is based partially upon how many users will be on the system; a user is called a "seat." A host of other factors also come into play, including how strategic the account is considered to be to the software company. Some software vendors, such as Arena Solutions or Demand Works, publish their price per seat directly on their website, but the vast majority of enterprise software vendors do not publish their prices. Instead, prices are given only after considerable interaction between the vendor and the company.

2. *The Consumer or Buyer Can Effectively and Efficiently Compare the Alternatives:* Unlike the consumer software market, the executives who make the purchasing decisions are never the same as those people who use the software. In fact, neither the executives nor anyone else at the company will actually use the solution prior to the purchase. Typically the potential customer will see a few software demonstrations or review some screen shots. Much of what is published about the software in marketing literature—or what is stated by vendor salespeople—is either false or not applicable to an actual implementation. Not understanding the distinctions between applications themselves, corporate decision-makers rely upon sales representatives, consulting companies, and analyst firms for this information.

3. *Sellers Do Not Have Monopoly Power:* In the enterprise software market, a number of vendors have monopoly power. This requires some explanation. A monopoly is one seller and many buyers. In real life there are few examples of this textbook definition of a monopoly; however, most companies can be placed on a continuum between perfect competition and monopoly. When an economist states that an entity has "monopoly power," this means that the buyers have restricted options and the sellers are in a good position to control the terms and evolution of the purchase. Monopoly power exists in the enterprise software market mainly because there is so little anti-trust enforcement in this market. For example, Oracle was allowed to purchase and essentially dismantle PeopleSoft, along with numerous other acquisitions. Acquisitions stem from a combination of financial strength and innovation weakness. When a smaller company has a better product than a bigger company, but the bigger company has more financial resources than the smaller company, the acquisition allows the bigger company to simply take over the smaller company. Acquisitions are critical to restricting competition and to reducing the degree of innovation in any field. Acquisitions prevent turnover in the leadership within the industry, and is almost universally bad for buyers. A major reason as to why the negative aspects of acquisitions are not discussed in the business press is that often the acquiring companies are also the biggest advertisers. For them there is no need to upset the apple cart. Software is subject to something called the "network effect," which occurs when the value of a service increases with the number of people using it. An example commonly provided is that of the telephone. The more people that have a telephone, the greater the value of any one telephone. Another good example is Facebook. The fact that so many people are on Facebook means that the value of Facebook is very high. This is intuitively obvious. However, the network effect also applies to consumer and enterprise software, and it applies to products and services that are not actually "networks" (the two examples of the telephone and Facebook clearly are networks). Microsoft Windows is the beneficiary of a powerful network effect, not because Windows is part of an actual network, but because applications must work with the operating

system, and software vendors want to write their products to work on popular operating systems. The same is true of hardware. Generally hardware manufacturers don't care which operating system runs on their hardware. However, they want their hardware to sell well and the best way to do this is to make it compatible with the most popular operating system. Windows used its monopoly power in operating systems to branch out in other directions, such as browsers and office software. In fact, the US Department of Justice case against Microsoft (which the Department of Justice won) was that Microsoft unfairly used its monopoly control over the operating system to also monopolize the browser market. Popularity creates its own credibility. Furthermore, companies prefer to buy software from the same vendors that produced the other software they currently use. There are a couple of reasons for this preference. The software that is used by companies must share data, and in theory, software produced by the same vendor should share data seamlessly. In addition, the act of purchasing software from a software vendor creates a relationship with that vendor. A perfect example of this can be found in the ERP software category. ERP systems can be considered the "mother ship" or foundational set of applications within a company. Almost every system acquired by a company must share data and be integrated with the ERP system. An ERP software vendor that sells non-ERP products (which in all likelihood are inferior to other software in that category) still has a great advantage over its competitors because the vendor can say that its product is better integrated to its ERP system than any other competing application. For this reason, as well as a number of other factors, vendors that provide the ERP software have a lock-in. Therefore, it is not at all surprising that the largest ERP vendors in the world (SAP and Oracle) also have dominant market share positions in many other software categories, as is shown in the following graphic for supply chain software.

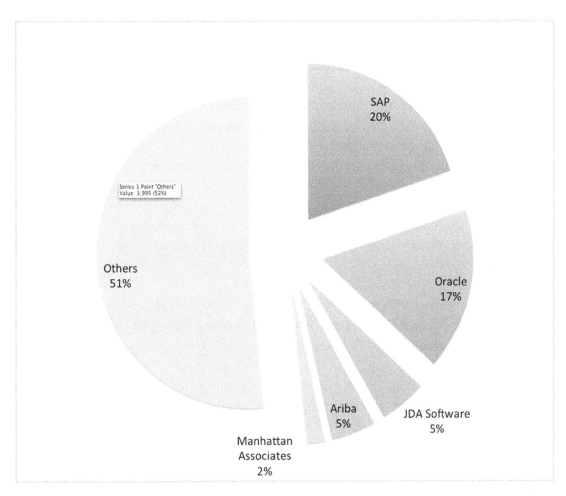

The graphic above shows that two software vendors control 37% of the enterprise software market for supply chain applications. SAP and Oracle are the heavyweights in multiple enterprise software categories.[2]

---

[2] This graphic was generated using data from Gartner.

The Most Important Thing to Take Away from the Enterprise Software Market

It is important to understand that much of the information necessary to make good software selection decisions in the enterprise software market is hidden from view. In most cases, to obtain this information you must contact each vendor directly, interact with them, and go through their process (which they control). Again, there are exceptions. For instance, some companies publish their prices right on their website. But, the information that is available from analyst firms tends to be quite high level, and there is nothing like "Consumer Reports" for the enterprise software market.[3] Information from consulting companies is highly biased. Furthermore, the vast majority of published information on various applications is promotional in nature and this includes books and Internet-based information.

Conclusion

In order to improve software selection outcomes, one must understand the incentives of all of the parties that are involved in providing information to buyers. This includes, vendors, consulting companies, IT analyst firms, and publications. That is, the first step to analyzing the information provided by various entities is to analyze the entities themselves. I have experience either working for or working with all of these entities, and know how they operate; however because I am an independent consultant, and work for none of them I am able to explain how they really work. Most authors cannot do this because they work for one of the entities, and would face repercussions if they were to publish the same material. This book has specific chapters dedicated to these entities as well as the information, they provide. However to begin, we will address the issue of software sell-ability versus implement-ability as this will set the stage for the later chapters.

---

[3] In the SCM Focus Press book *Gartner and the Magic Quadrant: A Guide for Buyers, Vendors and Investors,* I compare Gartner against *Consumer Reports* on a number of important and generally accepted research criteria.

CHAPTER 3

Software Sell-ability versus Implement-ability

In many parts of this book I explain how to make the software selection more about implement-ability rather than the sell-ability of the software. The reader will also understand why the marketing literature reads the way it does and why they need to ignore the "sell-ability" parts of it and seek instead documentation that reflects the "implement-ability" of the software. They will better understand the types of questions they need to ask of references, and check whether they consider the reference to be one the company provided merely to add to their "sell-ability." By understanding the difference between sell-ability and implement-ability, it's easier to understand where the real interest lies for the entities that provide information to the selection process.

Many pressures cause software to be developed into what you see as the final product. This information sets the stage for the end of the chapter, which will focus on how to select the most implementable solution. It would, of course, be quite nice if software were always designed to be functional rather than sold. Vendors have a limited amount of resources that they can apply to the development of their products. There is a general misimpression that software development occurs along the lines of what is desired by customers, which should lead to desirable outcomes. This sounds plausible enough. However, the reality of software development (and this applies to all enterprise software to varying degrees) is that there are competing agendas: not only the customers' agenda but also the vendor's and even those of third parties such as IT analyst firms. This problem is exacerbated at the larger software vendors where the strongest incentives exist to throw things over the wall. I recall having a discussion on this topic with representatives from the vendor PlanetTogether. I asked them why their software seemed so much more usable than other software in their software category, and one example they gave was that the company was just too small to throw things over walls and develop functionality that had little practical implementation value just to get a sale. The smaller the entity, the more affiliation each individual has with other individuals, the more they personally know them—can receive negative feedback for aggressively perusing one's personal agenda at the expense of others.

So far I have only explained the agendas internal to the vendor, however it does not end there. As explained in Chapter 5: "How to Use the Reports of Analyst Firms Like Gartner," because vendors want to score well in IT analyst ratings, they are under pressure to match the vision that the IT analysts have for their software category. The same issue applies for software investors. Software investors have a particular story that they find more appealing for investing. For instance, Adobe is well-known for its suite of design applications that includes Photoshop and Illustrator. However, Adobe decided to move to a SaaS-based solution, which meant that users now rent the Adobe creative products for a monthly fee. While there were several reasons for this change, one stated reason was to stabilize the company's revenues (moving to a monthly charge rather than seeing its revenue bunched up after their upgrades are released), thus making Adobe more appealing to stock analysts who prefer to see stable revenues. However, was this the best-combined solution if customer's interests were accounted for? Many people that use Adobe's creative products don't think so.

Even if we limit our discussion to just the vendor and buyer, there are multiple people in multiple departments who often have competing objectives. If we take just the vendor's competing objectives, for instance, one of the pressures comes from the need to have implementable software that buyers can actually use.

However, other pressures come from the need to sell software. The agendas of those who sell software and make software implementable may sound complementary, but in fact they are not at all complementary and are a major source of friction within vendors.

The Case Study of i2 Technologies

I once worked for a software company called i2 Technologies, which is a textbook example of what happens when marketing and sales completely co-opt product development. Not only did i2 Technologies come out with too many new product enhancements, they simply came out with too many new products. I2 Technologies fell victim to Enron Syndrome—too much confidence in one's innovation, too much focus on the stock price rather than the business, and accounting irregularities (necessary in order to keep continual improvements in earnings). Most of i2's best products were the first ones they developed, before the media created an echo chamber for them and Enron Syndrome took hold. I found out first hand as a consultant implementing projects the new products were universally the problem applications. Few of these products actually worked and it eventually brought down i2 Technologies, once a thought leader in its space. The company was acquired cheaply by JDA. I worked in consulting within i2 Technologies, and there was a great deal of friction between marketing/sales and consulting because we were not able to deliver reference-able accounts because the new software was essentially not implementable.

Functionality Creep

An important component of how companies rate software is how many areas of functionality the software includes, which in turn encourages vendors to add more and more functionality. However, this continually-added functionality also increases maintenance and quality problems. That is, it is easy for a software vendor to bring out more functionality than it can reasonably maintain. Vendors do this because Marketing and Sales repeatedly go to Development and say, *"If we only had this area of functionality we would get this big client."* Buyers who have purchased software already constantly ask vendors for adjustments to the software, and in most cases they are not willing to pay for these improvements but simply want them rolled into the next version of the software. However, buyers have a self-centered view of the software, only seeing the things **they want to do** in the software. Generally, they do not understand the vision of the software, and are mostly unconcerned as to whether or not other buyers are also interested in using the software in the same manner. In essence, clients would like to turn a software vendor into their personal custom-development shop, while vendors need to make sure that the functionality they develop can be sold to multiple clients. Sales and Marketing know what they can sell, but are frequently inconsiderate of how adding new functionality can negatively impact the maintainability of an application. Therefore, the buyer, sales and marketing, with their focus on adding functionality, have a much more limited view of the software product than does Product Management.

The product management process maintains this list of product enhancements (some driven by customers, some internally driven, some driven by sales), estimates how much the enhancements will take in terms of time and money, and prioritizes the enhancements that have the best potential to "improve" the software so that these are worked on first. I used the term "improve" in quotation marks because it is a subjective term. To sales, improvement means it will make the software sell better. To the buyer, it is something that will allow them to better meet their particular business requirement. To an implementation consultant, an improvement means the software will be easier to implement. To the product manager, "improve" may mean that the change is consistent with the long-term vision of the product. Therefore, the definition of the term "improve" very much depends upon who you are and your incentives and motivations.

The Dynamic Nature of Software

Software is like a living organism in that it is constantly growing and changing and has a certain life cycle. The lifespan of software is relatively short compared to other products, some reasons for which I have listed below:

1. Application software relies upon underlying layers. These layers include things like databases, operating systems and hardware. When these underlying layers change, the software must also change. For instance, if an operating system falls out of favor, the software must be ported to the new operating system. Software is designed to work on a particular category of hardware. When the hardware changes, the software must be rewritten. For example, there has been a movement from single-processing servers to

multi-processor servers. When this occurred, some vendors (particularly those who sell high performance applications) did not place porting multi-threaded processing high enough on the development prioritization list, so are still only using single processors.

2. Software is a rapidly evolving product category. Applications must be updated constantly or they become outdated. There can be classic cars—cars that you wish they still made—but classic software is really just uncompetitive software. If you were to go back and review software from a decade ago, you would notice that the software appears dated compared to current designs. In fact, much of the software we use has not been around that long, and while an application may have the same name as what was sold as the same product a decade ago, it is a very different animal.

3. Larger vendors often acquire successful and innovative small vendors. When this happens, the most common outcome is for the acquired vendor to stop being a leader in their category. The acquiring vendor simply procures the smaller vendor's customers and stops innovating with the product. Many of the employees of the acquired firm, particularly those most responsible for product innovation, leave the merged company. Acquisitions are in fact one of the prime causes of a software product becoming irrelevant.

4. Under constant pressure to add functionality, applications can become so high-maintenance and difficult to use that they lose their original benefit and become vulnerable to less complex products that work more efficiently. This phenomenon was recognized by the blogging platform WordPress. WordPress is the most popular blogging platform in the world, and powers many of the blogs and websites that we all read. I have been working with the software since 2007. This highly respected software is free and has grown enormously since it was originally introduced. Essentially, WordPress receives an unlimited number of requests to add functionality to its software. However, early on it decided to not develop the product to meet all of these requests, but instead to allow plug-ins. WordPress simply allows its software to interoperate with third party software vendors (most of them do not charge for the software they create), and in this way WordPress is not responsible for developing or maintaining those plug-ins. This system has been extremely successful and has allowed WordPress to continue to grow

with a seemingly unending number of plug-ins. WordPress is not distracted and instead can concentrate on what it does best, which is continuing to develop the core WordPress software. Unfortunately enterprise software does not work like this, and therefore can easily grow unwieldy under the new functionality, which results from constant requests for improvement.

Adjusting the Software Selection Approach to be Focused on Implementation

I have explained how software development and software vendors tend to work in order to help those who perform a software selection to account for these factors and to make better decisions.

The first thing that should be recognized is that the buyer will not implement all the functionality or get all of the functionality that they desire to work. A major strategy of vendors is to anticipate every need that a company could have by placing a very complete set of functionality in their applications. However, as this type of software tends to be difficult to implement, companies greatly overestimate their ability to implement functionality.

Software selections are often performed with the incorrect assumption that the buyer will place more resources on the implementation and maintenance of the implementation than they actually are willing to place. To use an example from my implementation experience, when companies select statistical forecasting applications they often are attracted to the functionality of complicated forecasting methodologies (mathematics that drive the forecast). They have much less interest in hiring and paying people with forecasting education and experience to actually run the applications. Some things can be done to simplify forecasting for individuals; however, they should be able to understand what the application is doing. Many forecasting applications have thirty different forecasting methodologies, yet at company after company I see only a few of these methodologies used. There is a way of automatically choosing among the different forecasting methodologies, and even though most companies cannot get this functionality to work, there are vendors for which this type of selection is automatic.

Secondly, there are many more practical areas of the forecasting applications that are just as important to the success of a statistical forecasting application, yet these areas are not emphasized during the software selection. One can't know what these areas are unless one was to implement and use the software oneself. This is a clear example—and just one of many examples—of how the buyer does not focus on what really matters in an implementation.

http://www.scmfocus.com/demandplanning/2010/09/why-companies-are-selecting-the-wrong-supply-chain-demand-planning-systems/

Making Realism a Priority

In the US during the past forty years, the bicycle has been transformed from a practical machine for transportation into a far less practical item that offers more ego-driven functionality (lower weight, aggressive styling, high turnover in design) and less practical functionality (ride-ability, safety, cargo capacity). The bicycle is an excellent example of the effect that marketing can have on an item's transformation. Marketing can tell a company what will sell, but they have no technical expertise to help a company understand what will work in practical usage. In fact, in most cases they undermine the design proposed by engineers or developers. If we take the example of the bicycle in the US from the perspective of usability, the redesign has been a failure. How can I say this? Well it shows up quite prominently in the distances these bikes are ridden per year. Luckily, research comparing distances ridden per country is available. Countries such as Denmark and the Netherlands are renowned for not riding US-style bikes and for retaining their older designs. A visit to Amsterdam will quickly make evident to the traveler that the styles used by the Dutch are completely different from those used in the US. The Dutch bike is known for its distinctive and traditional design. By having two countries with opposite bicycle designs and by comparing the frequency with which these bicycles are ridden, we can gain a good approximation of how effective the changes to the bicycle have been in the US.

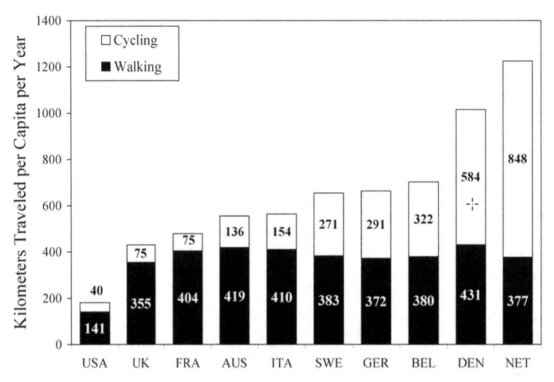

This is for the year 2000. And for that year, the average person from the Netherlands rode 21.2 times farther than the average American. In 2000 the US population was 281,421,906, while the Dutch population was 16,783,092. However, the Dutch as a country still cycled twenty-six percent more miles than the US.

This graphic really cannot be spun in a way that favors the US design of bikes. What is clear is that in the US, marketing influenced the design approach, which concentrates primarily on the "coolness factor" of the bicycle—that is a bike that is designed to be sold rather than ridden. This leads to a large number of bicycles that sit in the garage, not being ridden. In the US, the average bicycle is ridden forty miles per year at an average speed of just fifteen miles per hour (meaning that the average rider rides for two hours and forty minutes—over an entire year).

Furthermore it should be remembered that bicycles are a much easier "selection" decision than the selection of enterprise software. However, the transformation away from usability on these consumer items, which are tested directly before purchase, demonstrates how marketing and impracticality can affect product development.

Poor Software Selection as a Contributing Factor to the High Failure Rate of Enterprise Software Implementations

Finding the root cause for the high failure rate of enterprise software implementations has been the subject of much questioning. Poor software selection is one of the causes. In fact, while the reasons are elementary and quite easy to adjust, they will not be changed because this is simply how companies have chosen to operate and entrenched interests and ways of doing things often do not change.

Buyers are frequently more interested in factors outside of implement-ability and thus you cannot rely upon enterprise software to be designed for implement-ability. Some people have a hard time seeing why this is the case, the logic being that software that is not as implementable will eventually lose to those competitors with more implementable software. However, as I have explained earlier in this book, the enterprise software market is not an efficient market. There are many factors that drive buyer revenues, and the implement-ability of software is only one of the factors. As discussed previously, many large vendors have partnerships with large consulting companies. These large consulting companies recommend their vendor partner's software because doing so maximizes their revenues. Smaller software vendors will never enjoy this relationship with large consulting companies regardless of how implementable their software is. Software failures are hidden and the feedback loop about software's implement-ability is to a great degree broken.

Conclusion

While those in marketing will disagree, software cannot be optimized for both sales and implement-ability. Software that is highly implementable means that product management has accounted for the important enhancements but has not put every enhancement request into the product.

A major objective of the individuals who support a software selection effort is to ignore much of the marketing hyperbole and salesmanship and instead find the applications that offer the best combination of functionality to match with the buyer's requirements, while at the same time considering the implement-ability of that functionality. The buyer may not implement all of the functionality that they desire, and the implement-ability of the functionality is as important as whether or not the functionality exists in the vendor's application.

The overall theme of this chapter is that vendors have in many ways optimized their products to be sold rather than implemented effectively. Larger vendors are more prone to doing this than smaller vendors.

CHAPTER 4

How to Use Consulting Advice on Software Selection

Consulting companies are major influencers for enterprise software purchasing decisions. Usually, one of the major consulting companies is permanently resident as an enterprise software customer. The best place to start in understanding the advice provided by large consulting companies is to analyze their institutional structure. This tends to apply to small consulting companies as well. Understanding how consulting companies make their money is also critical to understanding how they work. As they say in political thrillers and investigative journalism, "follow the money."

There are several lines of thought regarding predicting behavior. One theory says that the individual can determine behavior of other individuals in an institution. History provides examples of this—that is, individuals who set their own agendas. However, the incentives of the institution are a more reliable guide to behavior. Individuals whose behavior diverges from the incentives of the institution tend to be short-lived in that institution. Therefore, while consulting companies are made up of a large number of people, their policy can be determined by both observing their incentives and by observing their output. Output is a far more predictive measurement than an institution's statements about itself because for the most part, an institution's behavior diverges greatly (and I mean this quite generally) from its statements. For instance, the worst thing that one could do to understand how an oil company works is to go to its website and take the statements it makes there at face value.

The Institutional Structure of Consulting Firms

Consulting companies have the following features, which are important to interpreting their advice on software selection

1. Consulting companies make their money based upon billing an hourly rate for their employees.

2. Their employees cannot be capable in all—or even a small percentage—of the software in a category. Because enterprise software is complex, ordinarily a consultant will work in both a single software vendor's application, as well as specialize in a single module within that brand. For instance, I work in SAP, which is the largest enterprise software vendor. I have worked in different modules, but I tend to get most of my work from a single module.

3. Therefore, they tend to have a deep specialization in a relatively small number of applications. Unsurprisingly, they tend to specialize in the largest applications. Specializing in a large and popular application allows a consulting company to get the highest percentage of billing hours out of their resources.

4. The people that make software recommendations to clients are called "partners." Partners are the senior management of the consulting companies. There are different levels of partners, with the most senior partners driving the policy of the consulting company. In fact, some of the policies (e.g., the policies regarding which major vendors they should focus on in their consulting practices) were decided long ago, and these policies are not decided or re-determined in any way periodically. People not familiar with the consulting market may say, "Wait a second. These consulting companies have many consultants at all different levels. Surely, when individuals

work for them, a variety of viewpoints are available to consulting clients." Actually no. This is a common misconception. The consultants below the partner level have no influence on what recommendations are made. The partner discusses what will be recommended with their consultants before meeting with the client. And this not only applies to full-time employees. When I have worked for consulting companies as an independent consultant (a so-called subcontractor) I was repeatedly pressured and told what viewpoints I should give the client. The advice I give must fit with the story that the partner wants to tell. However, they want to create the illusion that their opinion is my personal opinion. In fact, even the partners at the level I work with do not set policy. These policies, such as which software to recommend, are set far above the partners that actually work on projects, at the senior partner level.

5. The partners at the major consulting companies are very motivated individuals with very high compensation who must meet yearly consulting services sales quotas. In many ways, being a partner is a cushy job and the only people a partner really answers to is other partners. However, their yearly services sales quota hangs over them. In order to meet these sales quotas, they must place their consultants and this means selling or placing the consultants that have experience in the applications from the major software vendors (although consulting companies do occasionally place independent contractors on projects, they prefer not to as their margin on an independent consultant is much less than their margin on a full time employee).

6. Consulting companies are extremely hierarchical—I would say approaching that of a military organization. The resources below the partner level have no say in how the organization is managed. In fact, they don't even have a say on the technical recommendations that they make if they happen to contradict with the position that the partner wants to send to the client. If a recommendation is to be provided by a consultant, which may affect sales of consulting services, the recommendation will be run past the partner first. The partner will then tell the consultant what his or her "professional opinion" on the matter will be.

It should be relatively clear from the points listed above, but partners must be able to convince their clients to hire their consultants, who are trained in the applications from the major vendors. However, in order to convince their clients to staff their resources, they must also convince their clients to implement the software of the major vendors, as that is the expertise that their consultants offer. Thus, consulting companies have a conflict of interest when making recommendations regarding software selection.

To prove this, let's take a hypothetical example. Let's imagine a new partner joins IBM or Deloitte or any of the other major consulting companies (it does not matter which because they all operate in a similar fashion). Let's further imagine that this partner is truly focused on selecting the best software on the market to meet his or her client's requirements. An objective analysis would find that some of the best software available on the market to meet the client's needs is not the software for which the partner has trained resources. If the partner were "honest" and put the client's interests above his own, the partner would admit this fact to the client, increasing the likelihood that the client chooses a software vendor for which the partner has no resources that can be staffed. (At this point one might say that the partner could hire independent contractors to perform consulting, taking a lower margin on them. However, the contract market is well-developed for the major applications only, so for anything but the larger vendors, this is not an option.) As soon as the client chooses software, which the partner cannot staff, the partner loses out on both the services revenue and also their ability to control the implementation. If the client were to select an application from a smaller vendor, in most cases the consultants will come from that vendor as well. A partner that cannot staff as many resources on projects will eventually fail to meet their quota, and will be asked to leave the consulting company. Therefore, *even if a partner wanted to (and having worked with many of them I can say that most of them don't care either way),* they could not provide objective advice to their clients. This is the problem when any entity—not just consulting—receives a benefit if they advise a client to do one thing or another. This conflict of interest is rampant also in the financial industry, where recommendations are often made based upon the result that would maximize fees. Before moving on to the topic of how to interpret a consulting company's advice, I will finish off with a short story about how the large consulting companies operate.

I was at one time a manager at a large consulting company. During software training, I met a person who was in a management position at a company that was implementing the software I worked with. At the beginning of the training session we went around the room and stated the company for whom we worked. Once this person found out the company I worked for, he approached me and asked if I could pass on information to someone in my company about our support in selecting a consulting company for their implementation. I want to emphasize that this person was very clear that they wanted my company's help in selecting a consulting company, and not for actually performing the implementation.

I passed on this information to the partner to whom I reported. Because this was a fresh opportunity, I was besieged by phone calls from partners from around the country about how to handle the situation. One partner was of the opinion that the appropriate approach was to accept the consulting selection project under the false pretense that we would help them find the best consulting company for their needs, but in actual fact, we would impress them so much with what we had to offer that the client would simply call off the selection process and choose us instead. To carry out this partner's strategy, we would need to suppress information from the consulting companies that we were evaluating, but adjust the information so that it never seemed complete, and essentially stall the process so that the outcome would work to our advantage. It was not one rogue partner that recommended this approach, they all advised the same thing in one shape or form.

The selection phase of a project (be it software selection or implementation partner selection) is much shorter than the implementation stage and uses far fewer resources. Therefore, no consulting company that performs software selection and also has the capability and resources to perform the software implementation for a company will be satisfied with just the software selection work. In fact, a core strategy of every consulting company I have come into contact with is to use initial projects to gain larger projects. When I worked for KPMG I was told by a partner to snoop around for other work while I was there. Another partner used to repeat the phrase "penetrate and radiate" in meetings with large numbers of people and on conference calls (so it was not even a secret within the firm), so once into a client, you radiate through them by offering them more and more services. There is never even the pretense that services should be sold that the client actually needs—it is literally never even brought up in internal conversations. Consulting companies are generally unconcerned with whether these services are needed or appropriate, because at the end of the day it all comes down to billing hours, and the margin per hour.

Interpreting Information from Consulting Companies

One thing that I hope to establish is that all software selection information (and many other types of information) that comes from consulting companies is suspect. Depending on suspect information from consulting companies is one reason—and I will show many others—why quite often the software implemented by companies is inappropriate for their requirements. The software happened to be what the consultants that worked for the company were trained in and could bill for. Therefore, the software selected met the needs of the consulting company, but not the needs of the company making the actual software selection.

The misinformation provided by consulting companies for software selection goes beyond simply prompting their clients to choose software that is not the best for their needs. Consulting companies were instrumental in completely overselling the benefits of every major new software technology, with ERP being an excellent example of this. In the SCM Focus Press book, *The Real Story Behind ERP: Separating Fact from Fiction*, I cover the rather surprising result of my research that ERP has failed to live up to not just one, but also nearly all of the promises that were used to sell ERP systems to clients.

Consulting companies also misinform clients as to what they can expect in terms of the implementation effort, how well the software will work for them, and therefore their expected return on investment. When advising their clients, they follow a sales approach rather than a scientific approach. At times, the consulting companies I have worked for and worked with, as an independent consultant seem to be nothing more than sales arms for the largest software vendors (major consulting companies tend to have partnerships with only the largest software vendors). A good example of this was a webinar that I was asked to attend by one of my clients; a consulting company presented the webinar. I had worked with the application that was the topic of the webinar. However, throughout the webinar, this consulting company consistently presented a viewpoint about the application, one that I had never experienced even though I had worked on multiple projects with this software. According to this company, the application was "easy to install," "planners liked it," and "it just worked." Many of the statements they made were directly contradicted by my experience with this software on projects. However, when different companies that were logged into the webinar would ask a question, there was always a fast and easy answer for what could be done to mitigate the concern. The consultants who presented in the webinar were in full sales mode. They appeared to be willing to say anything in order to get the companies participating in the webinar interested in contacting them for consulting work. More detail on this experience is covered in the article, which I wrote on this topic and is available at the link below:

http://www.scmfocus.com/productionplanningandscheduling/2012/11/16/a-review-of-plan4demands-ppds-webinar/

Of course new implementations are all positive for consulting companies, as they provide the consulting services—they receive benefits with no risk. However, the implementing company takes a risk on every implementation. Therefore, the consulting company will have a strong tendency to be more Pollyannaish on the potential of the implementation than is warranted based upon experience. As an independent consultant I also interview to work as a consultant on implementation projects. From this experience I can say that there is simply no doubt that potential clients prefer to hear positive stories versus realistic stories regarding experiences with an application. So the consultants and consulting firms that offer the rosiest future scenarios have the highest potential to get the most work. This is of course not an isolated problem for software and consulting. Among lawyers it is well-known that those who paint a pretty picture to potential clients have a higher probability of getting more business.

Finding Entities That Lack Financial Bias

The only consulting companies that can be said to be without a financial conflict of interest are those that only perform the software selection and do not perform the implementation—if (and this is a big if) they are not resellers of the software. The same would be true of an independent consultant, although typically independent consultants are not hired to assist with software selection as this type of work tends to go to the large consulting companies that offer both software selection and implementation. However, while hiring an independent consultant or a consultant that only performs software selections addresses the financial bias, it does not control other types of bias. In my experience I have found many—if not most—of the consultants that work in my field have a strong bias toward the software that they work with. For example, at SCM Focus, I try to describe the reality of working with different software applications, and sometimes this means explaining the frustrating parts or poorly-designed parts of the application. There are several articles on the SCM Focus website about one particular application that had quite a few problems. I was actually contacted by a European independent consultant asking me not to do that, as it would decrease the demand for the application and by extension, his services. In other conversations, when I bring up some excellent functionality in a competing application and in my view, clearly superior functionality, the consultant will invariably say:

> *"Oh, well my application can do that. It may not do it the same way, but it does it."*

I will cover this in detail in Chapter 7: "How to Manage the Software Selection Process," but the fact that two entities can "do something," does not make them equal in doing that thing. I have observed that when the functionality is clearly inferior, the person defending the inferior product will use the term "different." I know of no other area of analysis where it would be accepted that because two items have something in common that they can be considered equal. For instance, both a bicycle and an airplane will get me from San Francisco to Los Angeles and the end result may be the same, but they are certainly not the same thing and they are not simply "different."

Therefore, if one is very careful, one can find entities in the market that do not have a financial bias. However, removing all bias is exceedingly difficult when contracting for consulting services. If someone who is advising you is to be taken seriously, at the very least they should not have a financial incentive based on your selection of a software application. Just achieving this modest goal would be a great improvement in the advice that you will receive over the current status quo.

Conclusion

Consulting companies are major influencers for enterprise software purchasing decisions. Consulting companies talk up their independence, but there is very little independence in decision-making or thought, particularly when a consulting company reaches any size. The evidence is that all of the major consulting companies make the same software recommendations. They recommend software that is from large vendors that they can staff themselves to bill the maximum number of hours.[4] This fact alone is a major reason why the enterprise software market is not competitive. The IT spend is misallocated in the system, and routed to less competitive offerings, and consulting companies are a major reason for this. Generally consulting companies also reduce the success ratio of enterprise software implementations. This is because so many applications that are selected are not the best fit for the client. In the vast majority of cases the application selected meets the business requirements to a much lower degree than other applications, which could have been purchased. Essentially contracting a large consulting company to provide selection advice is almost guaranteed to result in a bad software selection decision.

Large consulting companies are a bundle of conflicts of interest, and yet strangely, during the software selection process and while the consulting company is providing its "advice," this topic is not raised. The clients, as well as the consulting companies, all operate under the ludicrous assumption that the consulting company is actually looking after the client's interests. Large consulting companies want to limit all consultants from the software vendor because of both the desire to bill for the maximum number of consultants, and secondly, because having consultants from other entities on the project reduce their ability to control the account. This means having the project staffed almost exclusively by one's own consultants who are trained in just the applications from the largest vendors like SAP and Oracle. As soon as a smaller software vendor is selected, it means more non-consulting employees are working with the client. I was once at a consulting meeting with a group of Deloitte managers and one of them was complaining that they could not

---

[4] The lack of appreciation for this topic is quite shocking. If a person has 1,000 pounds of apples to sell, and no peaches, and they are asked which is better "apples or peaches," it's not hard to image which answer one will receive. Software buyers approach consulting companies that have just a few different types of fruit to sell, and thinking they will receive objective recommendations that will actually look at all of the fruit on the market.

reach their sales quota because the client had all these consultants working on the project that did not work for Deloitte and therefore they were not benefitting him personally. He had a strategy, which he shared with me, for getting these consultants from other companies off the project and replacing them with Deloitte consultants. One can imagine with these types of motivations continually working in the background how little any software recommendations from a consulting company has to do with what is the best choice for the client.

Both institutional analysis as well as my consulting experience support the fact that large consulting companies as well as most of the smaller consulting companies are making selection advice based upon their own revenue goals and that their client's interests do not factor into the advice they provide. The major consulting companies have hundreds of thousands of consultants working for them. A large percentage of them work in software implementation, with the more senior members working at least part time in software selection. However, not a single one of them can admit what is entirely obvious, that the software selection recommendations offered by their company has nothing to do with what is right for the client. Any consultant who did admit this either with a client or in any public forum would be quickly reprimanded and would either hurt their career, or they would simply be fired.

I have sometimes given advice to smaller software vendors, and on occasion the topic of working with a large consulting company to have their software recommended has come up. I have repeatedly told these software vendors not to waste their time courting large consulting companies. I gave this advice to one software vendor years ago, and they still scheduled a meeting with a partner from Ernst and Young. I attended this meeting. The message delivered from the Ernst and Young partner was that if this small software vendor brought a client to him, he would be willing to staff that project with his consultants. The small software vendor would have to train the Ernst and Young consultants in the application, and then they would bill the client at top dollar for a project Ernst and Young had not originated. That is the type of arrangement that small and even medium sized software vendors can expect from big consulting companies.

CHAPTER 5

How to Use the Reports of Analyst Firms Like Gartner

This is a short introduction about how to use Gartner. For the full detail on this topic please see the SCM Focus Press book, *Gartner and the Magic Quadrant: A Guide for Buyers, Vendors and Investors.*

Companies rely upon IT analyst firms in order to determine which software to buy. IT analysts are often relied upon to explain the state of the market to corporate software buyers. The most influential IT analyst firm is Gartner, and Gartner's most influential analytical product is called the Magic Quadrant.

An example of a Magic Quadrant is shown on the following page:

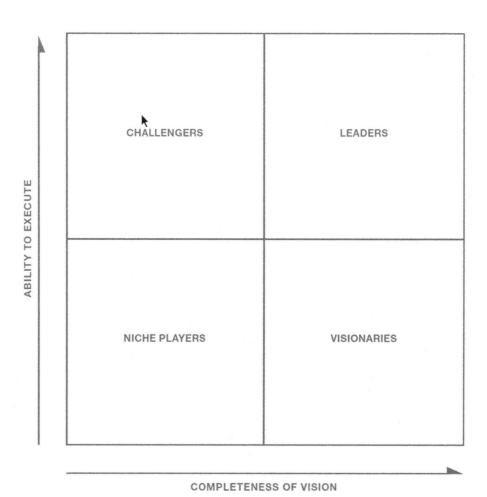

According to Gartner, *"Magic Quadrants depict markets in the middle phases of their lifecycle...."* Depending upon how the software vendor rates, they are placed into one of the following four quadrants. These quadrant descriptions are from Gartner's publication *Inside Gartner Research.*

1. Leaders: *"Leaders provide mature offerings that meet today's market demand. These providers also demonstrate the vision necessary to sustain their leading position as the market evolves. Leaders focus and invest in their offerings in ways that impact and influence the market's overall direction."*

2. Visionaries: *"Visionaries align with the Gartner view of how a market will evolve, but they have less-proven capabilities to deliver against their vision. In new markets, this status is normal. But in more mature markets, it may reflect a competitive strategy for a smaller provider (such as selling innovation ahead of mainstream demand), or a larger provider trying to break out of a rut to differentiate."*

3. Challengers: *"Challengers are well positioned to execute, but may not have a strategy in place to maintain strong, up-to-date value propositions for new customers. Larger providers in mature markets may often be positioned as challengers because they choose to minimize risk. Although challengers typically have significant human and financial resources, they may lack vision, innovation or overall understanding of where the market is headed. In some cases, challengers may offer products that dominate a large but shrinking segment of the market. Challengers have the opportunity to move into the leaders' quadrant by expanding their vision."*

4. Niche Players: *"Niche players do well in a specific market segment or they have limited ability to innovate or outperform other providers. This may be because they focus on a functionality or geographic region, or they are new entrants to the market. Assessing niche players is more challenging than assessing providers in other quadrants. While some niche players could make progress, others do not execute well and may not be able to keep pace with broader market demands."*

According to my interviews with Gartner, buyers should use the Magic Quadrant independently of Gartner's analysts. Furthermore, buyers should not interpret a Magic Quadrant as a recommendation to concentrate on those vendors that appear in the Leader quadrant. Gartner agrees that there is a misimpression that being categorized in the Niche quadrant is a bad thing. In fact, a vendor in a non-leader quadrant might be the best vendor for a particular buyer.

The Magic Quadrant Methodology
As has been previously stated, Gartner publishes only a high-level overview as to how it determines the Magic Quadrant rankings. People who read Gartner's analytical products, especially the most influential products, can only review a

high-level graphic, which is the output of the research. To find out more details and speak with an analyst, one must pay more, but Gartner does publish the criteria that count toward each axis. These criteria, quoted from Gartner's article *Magic Quadrants and MarketScopes: How Gartner Evaluates Vendors Within a Market,* are listed below.

Orientation of the Magic Quadrant Methodology

Something that was surprising to me (and is surprising to many people the first time I tell them about these criteria) is that only six of the fifteen bullet points (40%) are in any way related to the actual application offered by the vendor, which are the bullet points with two asterisks in front of them. Only two of the fifteen bullet points (13.3%) are ***directly*** related to the application. These are the bullet points with one asterisk next to them. However, these percentages are based simply upon an even weighting of the criteria. Gartner does not explain if they weight the criteria equally or not, so that is all I have to go by for this analysis. After reviewing many Magic Quadrants as part of the research for this book, it does appear as if the criteria are equally weighted.

Completeness of Vision Criterion

1. *"Market Understanding: The ability of a vendor to understand buyers' needs and translate these needs into products and services. A vendor that shows the highest degree of vision listens and understands buyers' wants and needs, which it can shape or enhance with its vision.*

2. *Marketing Strategy: A clear, differentiated set of messages consistently communicated throughout the organization and publicized through the Web site, advertising, customer programs and positioning statements.*

3. *Sales Strategy: A strategy for selling products that uses the appropriate network of direct and indirect sales, marketing, service and communication affiliates to extend the scope and depth of a vendor's market reach, skills, expertise, technologies, services and customer base.*

4. *Offering (Product) Strategy: A vendor's approach to product development and delivery that relate to current and future requirements.*

5. *Business Model: The validity and logic of a vendor's underlying business proposition.*

6. *Vertical/Industry Strategy: A vendor's strategy to direct resources, skills and offerings to meet the needs of market segments, including vertical industries.*

7. ***Innovation: Marshaling of resources, expertise or capital for competitive advantage, investment, consolidation or defense against acquisition.*

8. *Geographic Strategy: A vendor's strategy to direct resources, skills and offerings to meet the needs of regions outside of the vendor's 'home' or native area, directly or through partners, channels and subsidiaries, as appropriate for that region and market."*

Ability to Execute Criterion

1. ***"Product/Service: Core goods and services offered by the vendor that compete in and serve the market. This category includes product and service capabilities, quality, feature sets and skills, offered natively or through original equipment manufacturers, as defined in the market definition and detailed in sub criteria.*

2. *Overall Viability: Includes an assessment of the vendor's overall financial health, the financial and practical success of the relevant business unit, and the likelihood of that business unit to continue to invest in and offer the product within the vendor's product portfolio.*

3. *Sales Execution/Pricing: The vendor's capabilities in pre-sales activities and the structure that supports them. This criterion includes deal management, pricing and negotiation, pre-sales support and the overall effectiveness of the sales channel.*

4. *Market Responsiveness and Track Record: Ability to respond, change direction, be flexible and achieve competitive success as opportunities develop, competitors act, customer needs evolve and market dynamics change. This criterion also considers the vendor's history of responsiveness.*

5. *Marketing Execution: The clarity, quality, creativity and efficacy of programs designed to deliver the vendor's message, to influence the market, promote*

its brand and business, increase awareness of its products and establish a positive identification with the product, brand or vendor with buyers. This 'mind share' can be driven by a combination of publicity, promotions, thought leadership, word of mouth and sales activities.

6. **Customer Experience: Relationships, products, and services and programs that enable clients to succeed with the products evaluated. This criterion includes the ways customers receive technical support or account support. It can also include ancillary tools, customer support programs (and their quality), availability of user groups and service-level agreements.*

7. **Operations: The vendor's ability to meet its goals and commitments. Factors include the quality of the organizational structure, such as skills, experiences, programs, systems and other vehicles, that enable the vendor to operate effectively and efficiently."*

Gartner is of course free to use any set of criteria that they like. However, I find that few people actually read what their criteria in fact are, and most software buyers are under the impression that Gartner's ratings are much more product-focused than they actually are. In fact, most of Gartner's criteria are really just proxies for the size of the software vendor.

Gartner Report Adjustment Rules

Because a number of biases are present in Gartner's analytical products (which are both financial and non financial), it is important to adjust the Magic Quadrant, and other of Gartner's offerings in specific ways. I address how these biases can be demonstrated in the book, *Gartner and the Magic Quadrant: A Guide for Buyers, Vendors and Investors* and will offer a preview in the rest of this chapter. However, in this chapter I only explain how Gartner's ratings can be adjusted rather than the why this is the case with Gartner's ratings.

Never Use Just the Gartner Magic Quadrant to Make a Purchasing Decision

This point should be self-evident, especially if you have read the rest of the book up to this point. According to Louis Columbus, *"IT buyers regrettably sometimes make their entire purchasing decision just on the Quadrant alone."* It is hard to know where to begin as there are so many reasons not to do this, but as I have explained, Gartner's methodology for their Magic Quadrants includes factors that have nothing to do with the benefit to enterprise software buyers. Instead, the criteria are metrics that could be used by investors contemplating buying the software vendor's stock. Secondly, even Gartner does not want buyers or investors making decisions based simply upon the Magic Quadrant or any other research they produce. One should consider the research produced by Gartner as a "starter kit" to start the ball rolling for more analysis, contracting with Gartner for more analyst services, etc.

Adjust the Rankings for the Vendor's Size

Gartner prefers large software vendors. This large vendor orientation is clear, and it is difficult to see how a person doing a complete analysis on this topic could find that this bias does not exist. I hope that the analysis from Chapter 5: "The Magic Quadrant" has made that clear.

On the web there are several statements by Gartner analysts that Gartner does **not** favor large vendors. Other than managing perception, I can't think of a single good reason for anyone to say this. To believe that Gartner does not favor large vendors, one would have to both not understand the various Gartner methodologies and not read the Gartner research output.

A vendor's size is not a universal positive. Bigger vendors are less responsive, particularly if the buyer is not a large client. Because bigger vendors offer a broader set of products, they are constantly trying to capture more and more footprint within their existing clients, and they are not going to be happy selling a single application to a client. Larger vendors are less focused on their products, less focused on R&D, and more focused on marketing and on their partnerships with major consulting companies.

One of the reasons I enjoy keeping up with smaller best-of-breed vendors is because they have less bureaucracy, and they engage in far more innovation than the big vendors. I implement the software of the large vendors, and when I visit smaller vendors, I always feel as if I have traveled forward in time because the approaches we follow in SAP are so dated. I essentially implement approaches and technologies that are little changed from the mid-1990s. And of course, bigger vendors are more expensive (see the section on Adjusting for Price on page 51).

So, the bigger vendors in any Magic Quadrant are simply overrated by Gartner. The best way to account for this is by reducing their rating although I cannot provide a specific percentage adjustment.

Insert More Reality into Gartner's Ratings

Generally speaking, Gartner analysts do not have hands-on experience with the applications they are rating. Most of the Gartner analysts have at least fifteen years of experience in their area, so it is not that they lack experience but they usually lack implementation experience. Gartner analysts do speak with people in companies that implement software, but they speak at the level of CIOs and vice presidents. This constant interaction with senior executives at companies that buy enterprise software is a main reason why working for Gartner is considered such a good place to create contacts for future careers. However, these high-level people do not use the applications that they purchase; they pass along information to Gartner analysts that is already second-hand! While executives at buyers certainly know the problems that they face on implementations, overseeing implementations and actually working with the software are two different things.

Steps to Increase Reality of the Software Selection

Now that we have established that Gartner's ratings require more reality, the question is "how." An effective software selection will combine the high-level analysis provided by Gartner (provided either by reading research or by interacting with Gartner analysts) with more detailed analysis of:

- How the application actually works

- How the employees of the company will actually use the application

- How it will be configured and fit in with the rest of the company's footprint

Unfortunately, this is a lot more work and cannot be done by those who are the decision makers for the software selection. So, this more detailed work tends not to get done. However, it should be done—if not for all the applications under consideration then at the very least for the applications that the company finds the most intriguing. This applies to both buyers and investors, and is accomplished by having technical resources participate in the software selection process. I have no idea why so many executives think they are qualified to analyze statements made by presales consultants, but usually presentations are made to buyers with no one in the meeting from the buyer's side who can validate the technical statements made by the vendor's representatives.

Finding Technical Fact Checkers
Many times individuals with technical backgrounds can be pulled from the buyer's IT department. However, this is not always the case, especially if there is no one familiar with the category of application being analyzed. In Appendix A, I include a section on hiring independent consultants who can provide expertise that may not be available inside your company.

Viewing demos that are performed by a vendor's most skilled presales consultants is not a good way to truly understand an application. Rather than scripted demos, a more reality-based approach is to allow the reviewers to ask more questions and drive more of the demo.

Adjust Down the Rate of Predicted Change
As discussed in Chapter 2: "An Overview of Gartner," Gartner tends to overestimate the amount of change that occurs in any one software category, as well as the business developments in that category. Also, Gartner will describe industry trends as being more legitimate and permanent than they actually are. For instance, in my area, many companies have initiatives to move toward a make-to-order environment; however, because of the limitations of the approach most never will. This falls under the category of a "pipe dream."

It's easy to get the impression that because Gartner learns about these initiatives from senior executives within the buying companies, Gartner tends to take their word for it that most of these initiatives will succeed, when in fact a higher percentage may fail. This dynamic applies equally on both the buyer and the vendor side, as Gartner will frequently get on-board with a new technology initiative before a vendor and before that initiative has had the time to prove itself. For instance, in my field Gartner has been a major proponent of something called SAP Hana.[5] However, while the volume of the talk about Hana has been turned up for several years, I have yet to see its effect on any of my projects. I do not want to digress, as this is a separate and technical topic, but SAP Hana is really just something SAP should be doing anyway without a massive marketing offensive. It is simply a way to leverage evolving hardware and database technologies, and is really no big deal. In fact, I am surprised SAP and other vendors had not provided these options years earlier, as I began leveraging them myself on my own hardware several years ago. As I have stated previously, very little innovation happens at large software vendors. Small vendors put in the R&D and take the risk, and the large vendors copy the technology and crank up the marketing volume. When you control your customer base and have relationships with large consulting companies that recommend your product no matter its utility to their clients, innovation is simply not necessary. This is discussed in detail in the following link:

http://www.scmfocus.com/enterprisesoftwarepolicy/2012/03/11/why-the-largest-enterprise-software-companies-have-no-reason-to-innovate/

I have witnessed several innovations that no IT analyst firm has written anything about (one of which I covered in the SCM Focus Press book *Supply Chain Forecasting Software*). After a large firm has copied the technology, I assume I will read about how great it is in a Gartner report, maybe five years from now. In any case Gartner jumped on the Hana bandwagon while it was simply an experimental product. If Hana were released from a smaller vendor, it is highly unlikely that it would have been promoted by Gartner.

---

[5] The technology behind Hana is a huge yawn. It amounts to using solid state devices and new database structures that can handle very large data sets, and leverages SAP's database acquisitions to lock out Oracle from its accounts. In terms of the technology, these are things SAP should be doing anyway. A few years ago I ordered a laptop with a solid state drive because computers run better on them. I have also assembled multiple solid state drives in benchmarking tests of a planning system. However, I did not take out a press release after I did this. There are other areas of Hana, which are adjustments to the database design and that allow for faster table access. These are primarily for improving reporting speed.

As I hope the example above demonstrates, Gartner is well known for its Hype Cycle analysis, but Gartner itself will help drive a Hype Cycle to the "Peak of Inflated Expectations" (using Gartner's own Hype Cycle terminology). Often they are more swayed by how much "sense" a vendor's explanation seems to be over how it actually works in practice. Unfortunately, a lot of things seem like a good idea or seem to make sense but don't necessarily take flight. For example, SaaS was supposed to be the next great thing, but its adoption has been slow. Hypothetically, Gartner's frequent interaction with buyers should enable them to keep from doing this. However, my research into their past reports indicate that this is a consistent theme of Gartner despite their access to buyers that would allow them to validate vendors' statements.

Therefore, Gartner's reports should be adjusted and deferred. Whatever Gartner is predicting, it almost certainly will not happen as quickly as predicted. It should be understood that while many buyers may be moving in a particular direction, many will not be successful. Many initiatives are simply trends, and when they peter out, they are renamed. In my area, there is an initiative referred to as "lean," a rebranding of many identical initiatives of JIT (just in time), which mostly flamed out back in the 1980s. Lean is already running its course, and after it is not longer sellable, the consultants will come up with a new name for the same philosophies. There are now roughly half a million books on "lean," but the actual impact on inventory management?[6] Negligible. The benefit to consulting revenues of consultancies promoting lean concepts? Priceless.

Likewise, vendors frequently bring out new ideas and products, but most of these developments tend to be transitory and some are really just rebranding of old concepts by sales and marketing. Secondly, beyond time-phasing Gartner's predictions, many of their projections will never come to pass. When reviewing Gartner's past predictions, I found this repeatedly. Gartner's Hype Cycle proposes a consistent and eventual movement of technologies to the "Plateau of Productivity." However, some technologies or ideas are never implemented broadly and many disappear all together.

---

[6] Yes, I am joking. However, it is one of the most popular topics for publication in the supply chain management and production management space.

When No Magic Quadrant Exists

One of the biggest obstacles that a buyer or analyst can face is when there is no Magic Quadrant for the software category of interest. When Gartner decides to create a Magic Quadrant for a group of products or a software suite, it is impossible for a company that only makes a single product to compete in that type of analysis. Secondly, it is generally inadvisable for a buyer to implement multiple products from one suite. Doing this means using a vendor's weak products along with its stronger products, and in fact is the primary way that bad products are able to get sold. Without a connection to an ERP system, or as part of a suite, it is much more difficult for a bad product to get purchased. Also, once the analysis moves to the suite level, the business tends to get the short end of the stick, because at that point it simply becomes more about integration, and the functionality becomes an afterthought.

Nevertheless, software suites has been a common approach to IT implementation for several decades. While the concept was that there would be fewer integration issues if software suites were implemented, this approach has not meant the reduction in integration costs that were promised by ERP systems. This is explained in the SCM Focus Press book, *The Real Story Behind ERP: Separating Fact from Fiction.*

Furthermore, this has meant that the business does not get the software it needs. Software selection based on software suites does not emphasize each application, but instead emphasizes the suite. As explained in this quote from Christopher Koch of *CIO Magazine*, software suites themselves are mechanisms that reduce the competition a vendor must face.

> *"Indeed, integration standards interfere with ERP vendors' traditional ways of gaining and keeping customers and market share. Before the Web came along, your integration strategy was simple: Buy as many pre integrated applications from a single vendor as possible. That worked for you, and it worked extremely well for the vendor; integrated application suites fetched a high price and required long-term maintenance and support contracts that promised a steady, predictable stream of revenue from customers."* —ABCs of ERP

I have now seen many poor-performing applications implemented and a great deal of frustration on the part of business users and managers who were not delivered applications that ever had a chance of meeting their requirements. Such high-level Magic Quadrants are not useful to a company that is selecting an application that is a subcategory of that Magic Quadrant.

If a company is looking to select one or multiple products from a suite, it's difficult to see how a high-level Magic Quadrant of this type can be adjusted. Some detail about specific applications can be provided in the vendor description section, but this is simply not enough detail to support an informed decision. At this point, the Gartner analyst must be contacted, and there is little value that can be received from the Magic Quadrant by itself.

Adjusting for Functionality and Maintainability
Gartner employs analysts with a strong tendency to look at the bigger (biggest?) possible picture. Gartner looks at so many factors outside of how good the application actually is and how maintainable the solution is, that these most important factors are under-emphasized. Corporate buyers should strive to obtain the software that closely matches their business requirements and has the very best functionality. Gartner essentially tells buyers that the application is really just one component to the decision, but the problem is that Gartner has too many factors pulling their ratings away from practical software implementation criteria. This can be addressed by checking reference accounts and by asking the Gartner analyst how the various vendors performed on the surveys for functionality and maintainability.

Disregarding Gartner's Deeper Technology Insights and Predictions
In their reports, Gartner will sometimes make technology projections or try to describe the technology. I have found quite a few of these statements to be unreliable. Gartner shows no evidence of being predictive; there is no reason to pay attention to their predictions.[7] Furthermore, Gartner's technology prediction

---

[7] Gartner acquired a prominent IT analyst firm that specialized in my software category: AMR Research. Not only was AMR Research sometimes wrong, AMR was spectacularly wrong as I explain in this article, http://www.scmfocus.com/scmhistory/2010/07/how-analysts-got-everything-wrong-on-marketplaces/

opinions have been lampooned in numerous articles on the Internet, by authors who are experts in that particular category of technology. A number of the technology predictions I have read seem to have been designed to create a splash, rather than to stand the test of time. One that definitely sticks out as ludicrous was the prediction by Gartner that the Windows Phone would become the second most popular smartphone platform between 2012 and 2015 and account for 19.5% market share. 2015 is not yet upon us, but the Windows Phone has only 3.2% market share. Another example is taken from their prediction on SaaS, which is a quotation I also used in Chapter 2.

> *"'Up until now, the unique nature of the software market has meant that buyers had very little negotiating power after the initial purchase of a software license,' Gartner Vice President William Snyder said in a research note. 'We expect those dynamics to change considerably over the next 5 to 10 years, giving CIOs and software procurement officers more bargaining power while potentially reducing software vendor profit margins.'"*

> *"Gartner also predicts that a fourth of all new business software will be delivered by software as a service by 2011."*

Software costs have not significantly declined as predicted by Gartner. Gartner also overshot their second prediction that a fourth of all software would be delivered as SaaS by 2011. As of 2012, software delivered by SaaS represents only 4% of total software sales. Granted, SaaS software is less expensive than on-premises software, so the number of seats served is no doubt higher than its sales percentage. But it's difficult to see how the delivery of SaaS as a percentage of all enterprise software would be anywhere close to the 25% value of software delivery estimated by Gartner.

Was this bad analysis on the part of Gartner? Based upon the enormous advantages that SaaS has in terms of cost and time to deploy, as well as the efficiency of central administration by the vendor, I believe Gartner's projections were reasonable at the time. However, what many people who predicted a faster growth failed to consider were issues ranging from security concerns to the lower customizability of SaaS solutions, as well as the perception of integration issues that prevented SaaS from taking off as initially expected. The fact of the matter is that technology prediction is a difficult business. However, Gartner is not correct enough of the time for it to be taken seriously. Gartner has not demonstrated any special aptitude for technology prediction. On the other hand, if your client base does not notice Gartner's prediction track record, and if the bold predictions make for good marketing copy, then I suppose there is no reason to stop.

For those looking for technology predictions, Forrester has a better reputation for being right more often than Gartner.

Adjusting for Price

As discussed in Chapter 5: "The Magic Quadrant," Gartner does not account for price in their rankings. Instead they compare all products as if they are in the same cost category. This approach creates a bias toward more expensive products. In addition, because Gartner's methodology ranks larger vendors higher, Gartner's recommendation tend to push buyers to higher-priced products and products that result in higher consulting costs. (Larger vendors tend to have both higher acquisition costs and higher consulting costs.) Therefore, it makes the most sense to adjust Gartner's ratings for price. Unfortunately, this is not an easy task.

There are few software vendors like Arena Solutions and Demand Works that post the cost of their software on their websites. In fact, in many years working in the field of software implementation, I am rarely informed of the actual costs of the software being installed. Many vendors are cagey about their price; among a host of factors, the price depends upon the number of seats and how much the software vendor wants the account. Determining the actual costs is time-consuming and requires a significant amount of interaction with the software vendor so they can "understand their requirements."

Gartner is perfectly positioned to provide some type of rough approximation of the cost of the software, which could allow buyers to put some vendors out of their cost range. They are also well-positioned to estimate the consulting/implementation and maintenance costs of the different vendors per software category. However, if a company does not want to use a Gartner analyst to answer these questions, the company can adjust for Gartner's large vendor bias (and by extension their bias toward expensive solutions bias). They can push a smaller vendor up in consideration in order to account for lower cost and better value, if of course the vendor has other compelling factors. This leads to the next area of adjustment.

Adjusting for the Buying Company's Size

Gartner's bias toward larger vendors is related partially to Gartner's belief that companies prefer (or should prefer) to buy from the largest vendors. However, while larger buyers may prefer to purchase from larger vendors, it is less true of smaller buyers. Of course, Gartner's largest customers are the biggest companies in the world.

I do not know if smaller buyers would prefer buying from larger buyers if they could afford to do so, but the fact is that smaller buyers often can't. Generally small innovative vendors offer point solutions, have small deal sizes, and sell to small buyers. As the vendor grows, it is able to increase the size of buyers to which it sells. Therefore, Gartner's ratings fit the preferences (and checkbook) of large buyers far more than they do for smaller companies. Experience over time will let the smaller buyer know who they can afford to buy from, so for smaller buyers it is a simple matter to remove all or the majority of the largest vendors from their list and to focus on the other vendors.

Conclusion

While Gartner publishes reports, companies that buy subscriptions receive only a small percentage of their research. In order to maximize their revenues they prefer to deliver more information by having clients consult with analysts. The downslide to this of course is that consulting is more expensive. This chapter is designed to prepare buyers to work in a more cost effective manner with Gartner. One should consider the research produced by Gartner as a "starter kit" to start the ball rolling for more analysis, contracting with Gartner for more analyst services, etc. Gartner's research can be adjusted by adjusting downward the rankings for the larger vendors, as they are inflated. Secondly, as an implementer myself,

Gartner's research often makes me uncomfortable because it is at such a high level. In the software categories that are my areas of expertise, the analyst writing the report clearly does not have enough hands-on experience to explain the reality of the implementation issues that will be faced during the implementation, and a consultation with the analyst is not going to change their knowledge level. Gartner does a nice job of using surveys to uncover implementation challenges faced by clients with different software, but even still, this does not adequately find its way back into the Magic Quadrant ratings as my example of the highly problematic SAP BW product should demonstrate. This chapter explained how to add more reality into the software selection process, and I consider this to be one of the most important parts of software selection. Adjusting down the predicted rate of change is necessary because Gartner tends to overestimate this in their analysis. Initiatives are frequently announced with great fanfare, but most of them fail to find any purchase within organizations. Executives both overestimate the degree of innovation occurring within their own companies, and are naturally persuasive individuals, which is a major reason they have the positions that they do. Gartner often appears to be drinking the Kool-Aid, which is served by the buyers they interview. However, there is an optimism bias as the executives will always be confident of new initiatives within the company. Gartner's Kool-Aid drinking extends to vendors as well, particularly large vendors.

Another area that must be adjusted is functionality and maintainability. Gartner underestimates the importance of both of these dimensions of software implementation. The functionality is critical to the ROI and probability of success of the implementation. Because Gartner underemphasizes functionality, it has the consequence of promoting the purchase of riskier applications. In terms of maintainability, Gartner had clear evidence of the maintenance problems with SAP BW, yet they continued to list SAP in the leader quadrant. Certainly, the fact that SAP is the largest business intelligence software vendor makes them a "leader" in terms of their market share—and this is of course quite important to investors. However, it's unclear how simply having a large market share helps an application be maintained by a buyer. If the lowest quality offering, an application with very significant implementation and maintainability issues can be listed in the Leader quadrant, then Gartner's Magic Quadrant must be adjusted by buyers because these dimensions are of more importance to the buyer than they are being weighted by Gartner. The price of applications, therefore, must be adjusted by buyers. Gartner does not rate either the actual application cost, nor the TCO in the Magic Quadrant, so the most expensive solutions are placed on equal footing with the least expensive. However, the price is important to buyers and therefore, looking at a Magic Quadrant without adding price into the equation would not make much sense.

CHAPTER 6

How to Use Information Provided by Vendors

Software sales is known as one of the more aggressive types of sales. Good software salesmen are highly compensated, and are given every incentive to sell as much as possible. In some cases, such as a software company for whom I worked called i2 Technologies, the salespeople were so out of control in their lust to sell that they actually derailed the company. This orientation began at the very top of the company. The head of sales for i2 Technologies was famously to have remarked in a highly-charged sales meeting (all i2 sales gatherings tended to be highly-charged affairs):

> *"I never want to hear the excuse that software does not exist as reason to not sell."*

Information about software comes from either sales or marketing. Marketing includes the development of collateral materials, both printed materials and the website copy, which are designed to put the company's products in the best possible light. Both sales and marketing are under a great deal of pressure to compete with statements and literature provided by other companies. A big part of sales and marketing is about creating a vision, which has nothing to do with communicating real features in software.

Marketing Literature

Software vendor marketing literature can take the form of pamphlets or website copy, and can be quite easy to get hold of. This literature is very influential in software selection but, depending upon the vendor, often contains false information and is unreliable. For example, I have read numerous marketing documents that explain how a product performed "inventory optimization" (a particular set of mathematics for supply planning), when the software discussed did not actually possess this functionality. The videos below explain more.

http://vimeo.com/14844814

http://blip.tv/scm-focus/google-search-for-misuse-of-inventory-optimization-4122062

To provide further examples and explain what I mean, I have extracted quotes from some marketing literature. Below are some lines from SAP's marketing literature on their product NetWeaver, called SAP NetWeaver, interspersed with my critique on their statements. My critiques appear so frequently because the falsehoods are so prevalent throughout the document.

> *"The SAP NetWeaver technology platform is a comprehensive integration and application platform that helps reduce your total cost of ownership (TCO)."*

NetWeaver is not actually a product but a marketing construct; it is simply nomenclature added on to existing, mostly IT infrastructure, products thus making this statement untrue. As is covered at our companion site, Software Decisions, SAP has the highest total cost of ownership in any software category in which it offers a product.[8]

---

[8] The Software Decisions website is available at http://www.softwaredecisions.org

"It facilitates the integration and alignment of people, information, and business processes across organizational and technological boundaries."

No, it does not. NetWeaver only relates to infrastructure, and does not help out a client in areas outside of infrastructure, and not to belabor the point, but NetWeaver is itself not a distinct product.

"SAP NetWeaver easily integrates information and applications from virtually any source."

No, it does not. None of the products that were placed within the "NetWeaver umbrella," which relate to integration, the most prominent being SAP PI[9], enables integration any easier than other integration products. In fact, SAP PI is not even competitive with other applications in the same category. Companies primarily buy SAP PI because they either can't differentiate good integration software from bad integration software, or they think that they will be able to leverage SAP-to-SAP integration capabilities. Those individuals familiar with both applications would not support the idea that SAP PI is competitive with enterprise integration products such as Informatica. In fact, SAP misrepresents application integration completely with this sentence. Integration is always work—files must be transformed and converted to match with the data requirements of the receiving system. Jobs must be setup to carry the data from one application to another, and it must be scheduled in a way to run automatically. No application has been developed that makes integration "easy" anymore than a battery has been developed to easily store power. In fact, SAP PI makes application integration more difficult than other vendors. This should not be surprising, because ERP vendors have no special knowledge or ability to develop superior applications in this area. Application integration, like power storage, is always complex, and both have proven immune to magical promises about how transformative they would be. Vendors, not just SAP, have been pitching easy integration for decades now,

---

[9] SAP PI stands for "process integration," but it is really just an integration application. It was misnamed for marketing reasons.

and integration still is problematic, and still consumes a consistent percentage of the IT budget of buying companies.

> *"It interoperates with and can be extended using the primary market technologies—Microsoft .NET, Sun's J2EE, and IBM WebSphere. SAP NetWeaver is the technical foundation for mySAP™ Business Suite and SAP® xApps™ and ensures maximum reliability, security, and scalability, so your mission-critical business processes run smoothly."*

This is the technical gobblygook portion of the document. The intent here is to throw so many terms at the reader (who is typically an executive and is not familiar with these technologies) so that they will be impressed. It is also very unspecific about how this would all work, so the reader has to take the author's word for it. Many of the terms that are used in this quotation are already no longer relevant. I have already addressed the fact that NetWeaver is a meaningless term. The term "mySAP Business Suite" is no longer used, but it never was anything beyond a collection of other SAP products. The xApp program was a "brand" that held out the potential to smaller vendors of getting into SAP projects. In fact, the xApp program was a giant competitive intelligence operation, which allowed SAP to take intellectual property from other vendors in order to bring out competing products. I called for the xApp program to be discontinued or investigated by the Federal Trade Commission shortly after it came out, as the article below describes.

http://www.scmfocus.com/inventoryoptimizationmultiechelon/2010/01/its-time-for-the-sap-xapps-program-to-die/

However, the xApp program is now, in fact, dead.

> *"This Web services-based platform offers a comprehensive, tightly integrated set of capabilities. And by providing preconfigured business content, SAP helps reduce the need for custom integration and lowers your TCO."*

I work on SAP projects for a living, and this document is a few years old now, but I have never seen any of these "products" used on a project. I never saw any "pre-configured business content" and have never heard of this term used by anyone on any project at any time. SAP still has some of the highest integration costs of any application vendor because of the nature of their data backend, which does not allow the underlying relational database to be directly addressed. As I stated several paragraphs ago, SAP has always had the highest TCO (total cost of ownership) of any application I have reviewed, and continues to have the highest TCO.

> *"Enterprise Services Architecture is also a blueprint for complete business integration. Regardless of the functional or technical barriers and isolated applications that may have grown up over time in your company, Enterprise Services Architecture brings back flexibility, allowing you to design complete solutions that span all people who participate in your value chain, all information that is relevant to you, and all systems that are involved for each business process or problem. This means that you can now respond to workers' needs for business processes that are driven by collaborative, knowledge-based, and team-based processes rather than by isolated applications."*

No, it isn't. Not only do the products that pre-existed "NetWeaver" and were then added under the NetWeaver umbrella, not have the magical properties described in this quotation, they are not even competitive products. Workers in companies where SAP has been implemented do not have more responsive systems than other environments; they have decidedly less responsive systems. The last part of the quotation is pure hyperbole.

In one part of the document, SAP breaks down the benefits of NetWeaver by the different areas:

> *"Portal infrastructure—Gives workers unified, personalized, and role-based access to heterogeneous IT environments. Increases the efficiency of business processes spanning customers, suppliers, partners, and employees."*

SAP has been trying to get its portals used for more than a decade now, and they are still not used. SAP has a portal, but the potential that companies will benefit from it is low if they don't use it. Now I almost never hear about portals on projects.

> *"Knowledge management—Manages and makes accessible unstructured information such as text files, slide shows, or audio files. Includes integrated search, content management, publishing, classification, and workflow capabilities, as well as an open framework for third-party repositories."*

SAP has a product called Solution Manager, which has a few advantages in terms of documenting the implementation and allows Solution Manager to take you directly to configuration within the application. I analyze Solution Manager in the article below:

http://www.scmfocus.com/sapprojectmanagement/2012/01/the-end-of-sap-solution-manager/

However, these other things described in this quote either do not exist or are so overstated that they do not communicate what SAP's knowledge management products use. Furthermore, Solution Manager is really only used (and lightly used at that) by configurators like me. Solution Manager is not used in the way described above and no other portal, which SAP may offer to clients, works in that way.

> *"Business intelligence—Enables organizations to integrate, analyze, and disseminate business-critical information. Includes a robust suite of tools for creating and publishing customized, interactive reports and applications, which supports your decision making at every level."*

Business intelligence, which is covered by SAP's BI and Business Objects products, is not any more robust than any other reporting platform. In fact, according to the research firm Gartner; SAP has the lowest scores for both software quality and customer support of any application vendor in the space. I rarely see SAP BW add value for clients; in fact in most cases BI reports are missing in action.

> *"Master data management—Promotes information integrity across the business network in heterogeneous IT environments. Provides services to consolidate, harmonize, and centrally manage your master data, including business partner information, product master and structures, and technical-asset information."*

SAP brought out a master data management product called MDM. However, it never gained much of a following and had many implementation problems. It was not competitive with other master data solutions in the marketplace.

I could go on and on about SAP's marketing documentation, but hopefully you get the point. And while SAP takes enormous liberties with the truth, most vendor marketing documentation is in some way misleading. In fact, aside from entertainment value, there is little reason to read SAP's marketing literature. However, this is not always the case with all vendors. For instance, a vendor whose marketing documentation is quite accurate is Arena Solutions, a vendor that makes bill of material management software and for which I wrote a book that featured their software. I have never read any documentation from Arena that seems "off" or misrepresentative, and in fact a very good amount of Arena's documentation is quite educational. This is in fact what marketing documentation should be, but is very rarely the case because most companies cannot resist embellishing in order to make their case and to persuade in the hopes of selling more software. Let's review some of Arena's statements from their marketing literature to see how it differs from SAP.

> *"Item management is easy when part data, assemblies and documents—including drawings and data sheets—are all in one place. Give your team and designated suppliers controlled access to all the information they need to design and manufacture your product.*
>
> *A centralized product record allows your team to make faster and more efficient design decisions—like reusing part specifications from old designs—and save time and money."*

This is all true. When all information is in one place it's easier to find, and in fact Arena's software does just this. Arena's product also significantly increases the reuse of old designs. Observe that the hyperbole of these statements is minimal, and when contrasted to the highly-generalized statements that SAP made in their marketing literature for NetWeaver, these statements are quite specific. Arena is not saying their software will do everything, but that it will do something specific, and then explains how it will do that thing.

> *"Create a unique record for every part in your item master with customizable part numbering schemes and categories. Customizable categories can be used to determine the layout and sequence of fields in your part record. With up to **250 customizable attributes** per category, BOMControl allows you to record and track the data you need, at big-picture and granular levels."*

Again, more specifics are provided by Arena of what they can do. Arena's application can hold up to 250 customizable attributes per category. A person who works in this area should have no problem understanding exactly what this means.

> *"Immediately see what's changed in any version of your bill of materials with a simple toggle to Redline mode.*
>
> *Stop wasting time with phone calls or notes explaining every small change you've made to your BOM. When you grant supplier access to your contract manufacturers, they can see for themselves exactly what you've modified and how it impacts the overall product.*
>
> *Quickly compare multiple BOMs to see what has changed, or what is different. Optimize procurement and production with side-by-side bill of materials comparisons that reveal component needs across multiple product lines."*

These statements tell the reader quite a bit. They explain how a company can stop wasting time by leveraging Arena's functionality with regard to managing revisions. The BOM can be compared to see what has changed and procurement and production can be managed by component need across multiple product lines.

This is just a sampling of Arena's marketing literature of course, but all of Arena's literature reads this way. One can learn a lot from reading Arena's literature because they describe a reality, not only of their software, but also of the environment in which their software is implemented. On the other hand, it is very difficult to learn by reading SAP's marketing literature (and the marketing literature of many other vendors) because they are so busy selling, that they have no time or space to educate. SAP's explanations are absolutely overwhelming, as if they are attempting to include as many accolades as they can. They attempt to sell the reader *in every possibly sentence* instead of selling the reader on the overall paper. In fact, SAP's marketing literature is insulting to one's intelligence and to one's time. SAP marketing literature is not much read as it is "parsed."

How to Read and Differentiate Vendor Marketing Literature

In addition to learning from vendor marketing literature, there are more benefits. For example, more often than not, vendors who engage in extreme exaggerations and hyperbole are problematic vendors who are selling "pie in the sky." The marketing literature is telling you something about the company. The company who is ready and willing to sell you a bunch of baloney and has no standards for truth in their documentation will have a strong tendency to behave that way in other parts of the company and in their dealings with you. By reading between the lines of their literature, you can learn to steer clear of these vendors.

In addition, misleading marketing literature impacts the sales and presales groups of software vendors. Individuals who work in sales and presales rarely get first-hand experience with the application. Much of what they know about products comes from the marketing literature. They don't spend the time to talk with consultants who implement the software to determine what is true and what is not, and learn to be as accurate as possible. Most individuals simply don't care. If the marketing literature says that the vendor has developed a time machine, the sales group is going to go out and sell time machines. And of course as a buyer, it's your job to steer clear of companies selling time machines.

The Demo

The software demonstration (or demo) is one of the few opportunities to get first-hand experience with the software. Most information on demos (and there is not a lot to be found) explains how to put on a good demo. However, I could find nothing on how to get good value from a demo if you are the software buyer. There are several issues that negatively affect how accurately demos can be said to represent reality. However, from the perspective of buyers, the weaknesses of demos are that they tend to be artificial and are controlled by the vendor.

The common issues with demos are listed below:

1. The company's presales consultant typically runs demos. The demo is not an accurate representation of how the software will actually be used because this person specializes in knowing all the ins and outs of the software and is typically quite specialized in that application. Users will never attain the ease-of-use demonstrated by the consultant because they use several applications throughout the day and won't gain the same depth of knowledge about the product as the consultant. Therefore, the consultant's level of knowledge allows them to make the product look much easier to use than it really is, and to gloss over its imperfections.

2. Demos use dummy data, which provides a great deal of flexibility to the presales consultant who drives the demo. Applications run faster and more smoothly with smaller data sets.

3. Demos tend to be tightly controlled in that they follow a script. The script makes the application look much more fluid and fully featured than it actually will be when implemented.

4. Too often the users are excluded from the demo, meaning that the demo tends to be a high-level affair. However, it is the users who ask the most pertinent questions related to how the software would be used in an everyday setting.

5. The same bullet point above applies for technology resources. They are needed to ask questions related to how the software actually works under the covers, how it loads and updates data, makes decisions, etc.

6. Demos tend to be short. Most range from between forty-five minutes to an hour. This is not enough time to explore an application, particularly if it is complex. Large audiences tend to shorten demos because the demo is often seen as just one part of the presentation that day, and the more senior members tend to want to spend an hour on several occasions going over software. This short exposure time to the actual software is a mistake because the shorter the demo, generally the more the vendor can hide.

7. While I have never heard this mentioned in other published material on software selection, I find it very useful to have screenshots sent of interesting functionality. Once a buyer has screen shots they can mark up the screenshots, and then compare and contrast to screen shots of other applications. Comparing and contrasting functionality in this way is something I do when I chose software to showcase in books. This can allow a software selection document to be created that really explains the specific differences between the different vendors.

However, demos are extremely important. While it should be remembered that the vendor would like to control the demo, ultimately, the *buyer* is in control of how the demo progresses—*if the buyer wants to take that control.* It is the buyer's time that is being taken and the purpose of the demo is to inform the buyer if this is the right application for them.

The best way to take control of a demo is to declare how you would like the demo to run, and to do so well in advance of the vendor actually making the presentation. Without this communication prior to the presentation, the software presales consultant can legitimately say that she is not prepared to perform the demo in that manner. This is because demos must be prepared both in terms of the data that is used and how the presales consultant manages the demo. Most presales consultants are not comfortable with individuals from the buyer navigating through the application himself or herself, so they must be told beforehand if these individuals would like to do so. However, this can be accomplished even if the demo is not performed in person because all screen-sharing applications allow transfer control of the computer to anyone who is part of the screen sharing session. Another way of taking control of the demo is to stop the flow of the presales consultant's presentation. The presales consultant may have a set of things he wants to show, and plan on leaving questions until later, but this is a way of taking control of the demo. As a buyer, you should remember that the entire purpose of the demo is for you to understand whether this software should be selected. Therefore, the presales consultant's desires must rank as a distant second to the buyer's needs.

Ways to make demos more useful to the buyer can be determined by working backward from the limitations of demos:

1. The presales consultant can explain the software, but someone else should drive the demo, at least for part of it. By doing so, you are controlling the presales consultant's skill level. Yes, certainly a presales consultant can move very quickly between the screens, but how intuitive is the application for a first-time user? If I take the example of SAP versus Arena Solutions, SAP allows companies that have included SAP in their software selection process to view their software only through the presentation of a software consultant. Arena Solutions allows anyone to self-navigate through their online demo environment for thirty days. This speaks to the confidence level that Arena Solutions has in its software and its usability. SAP would never allow this because the difficulty in using SAP could become apparent. Not all companies have an online demo environment like Arena, but still, when a demo is presented the request can be made to have someone from the buyer actually navigate the software under instruction from the presales consultant, or the buyer resource and the presales consultant can take turns running the application. The more usable the application, the more open the vendor will be to getting the maximal exposure to the application for the buyer.

2. There is nothing wrong with allowing a presales consultant to start from a script. There are some things that need to be shown; however, the entire demo should not be from a script. It makes little sense for most of the demo to be "canned" or from a script as the standard things the vendor wants to show should be available for multiple viewings in video format on the vendor's website. At this point, the demo should center on things that the client has asked specifically to see (in advance) and the vendor should have built the demo specifically to answer these questions. Demos can also be

made more interactive simply by driving the demo with questions. Presales consultants are under a lot of pressure from the sales team to provide short and smooth demos that leave the buyer with a good impression. However, if it is explained that the buyer does not desire this, typically the demo can be driven differently.

3. Users need to be included in the audience during the demo, and their opinions should be solicited after the demo. Would they personally want to use the software? They should also be told to ask questions whenever they see fit and not at the end of the demo only. Users will pick up on things that executives will not. There is absolutely no logic to exclude the eventual users from a demo. When I worked at i2 Technologies, I recall that on one account the presales and sales team convinced the potential customers to keep users out of the demos. The sales and presales team explained to me that they knew the particular software they were showing was weak and that they would not be able to answer users' questions, so they needed to, in their words, *"sell directly to the top."*

4. Demos should be lengthened. A demo lasting an hour or less, or even multiple demos lasting an hour or less, is not sufficient to really understand how the application works in a variety of circumstances. The shorter the demo, the less representative the demonstration, and the easier it is to cover up weaknesses in the application. After the salespeople and the implementation consultants are gone, what will remain is the software. The software needs to work as the company desires and needs to be able to stand on its own and work efficiently the way the users need it to.

The SAAS/Cloud Vendors versus On-premises Vendors for Long-term Software Evaluation

Most enterprise software that is sold is called "on-premises," meaning that the software is installed on the servers of the buyer and is managed by the buyer. With SaaS/Cloud, the buyer does not actually install any software. Instead, the buyer receives the right to use the software that is installed at the vendor's location. There are a number of advantages and disadvantages to this approach; however one of the major advantages is that companies that offer their software as a SaaS/Cloud solution are in a very good position to offer trials of their software. However, only around 4% of all enterprise software is delivered as SaaS at the time of this publication. Some companies like Arena Solutions allow companies to test drive their software for thirty days by logging into their demo environment. However, other SaaS vendors do not offer this service. For instance Data Alliance, an SaaS vendor that I was analyzing recently, chooses to follow the on-premises model of presenting demos to potential clients, even though they could easily provide an SaaS demo environment for companies to test drive at their leisure.

Interpreting the Vendor-presented Story on Integration

Software vendors habitually present integration of the application as simpler and less expensive than it is in reality. This is true of both vendors selling a product that integrates to another product that you already own, or a suite of products from a single vendor that has prebuilt adapters (although not necessarily comprehensive adapters) between the applications to companies that provide point solutions.

Of all the information provided by vendors to software buyers, some of the biggest misrepresentations exist in the portion of the presentation devoted to integration. When I worked for i2 Technologies during the late 1990s, the sales people out of the Singapore office told their clients that XML would handle the integration between the i2 applications and other applications that the company already owned, as well as between i2 applications and applications outside of the company. I spent a good deal of time explaining to executives in i2's Asia client base that XML was just an integration document format, and not an actual integration harness. This was at the height of the XML craze. Then I noticed that the sales team had begun to insert the term "Java API" into sales presentations. API stands for "application programming interface," and this API was written in the Java programming language. Java API was supposedly better than an API written in the C language because it would be platform-independent. The problem was I didn't recall us actually implementing projects with a Java API. It became apparent to me that the integration development group would say anything to sales, and sales seemed to be putting things in the sales presentation slides because the customers responded favorably to our "forward thinking," regardless of whether our product actually worked that way.

If you attempt to dispute how the integration will work in practice, the vendor can always bring in someone more technical than anyone in your IT organization. This person will use a wide range of technical jargon to explain how smoothly your integration will be. It won't and there is little point in debating the point, but evidence indicates that integration will consume about the same amount of resources as it is currently consuming. Another story in the integration pantheon relates to SAP. In sales presentations, SAP misrepresents the comprehensiveness of the adapters they have built between their own products. The executives come out of SAP sales presentations thinking prebuilt adapters cover them if they choose SAP. However, if they were to check the adapters, he or she would find that the adapters do not cover all of the company's requirements.

SAP is a very large enterprise vendor, and many smaller vendors attempt to improve their marketability by becoming "certified" SAP, which amounts to the vendor submitting to the certification process where a minute amount of data is moved between two systems. After the fake test is passed, the vendor gets a certification badge that they can put on their website to improve sales. Outside of the marketing effect, there is little, if any, technical benefit to the implementation as I explain in the article below:

http://www.scmfocus.com/sapintegration/2011/11/15/what-are-saps-vendor-integration-certifications-worth-on-projects/

I have sat through many presentations on applications integration and have heard about all manner of Star Trek-like integration technologies, and yet integration works about the same as it did when I began working in IT consulting many years ago.

Client References

References are important not only for the initial software selection, but also to learn what functionality to enable in applications that are already owned. Vendors will often build functionality into applications that is either never accessed or infrequently accessed by clients because the functionality is not very good or is too high in maintenance.

Here are some of the reasons as to why software vendor references have limited usability.

1. Generally speaking, the vendor will supply only references who are satisfied with the solution (although I have heard of a number of strange stories where the reference provided by a vendor did not implement the software the vendor said they did, but the vendor still provided the reference). Reviewing vendor references sometimes gives preferential treatment to larger vendors who have more implementations under their belt, and that means more of their functionality has been implemented "someplace."

2. Companies that have agreed to provide references for a vendor typically feel some obligation to that vendor for no other reason than the relationship that they may have with their vendor consultants or vendor account rep. This same interpersonal allegiance is at work when clients co-present with vendors at conferences. Not wanting the vendor to look bad, the client sometimes stretches the truth in terms of how well the software is working. I have personally seen this happen at several conferences where I knew the state of the implementation and it bore no resemblance to what was actually presented.

3. I suppose I am naïve, but I was surprised to learn that vendors and consulting companies may on some occasions pay their references to provide them with a reference.

4. The reference that is provided oftentimes will not have completed their implementation, or the implementation may be so new that the reference account is unsure as to what they actually have. Vendors are quick to declare victory because they know good references can drive sales.

5. Implementing companies are very reticent to admit that a software implementation has gone badly. I am aware of a company that has been implementing two applications for roughly ten years, and has yet to get much functional use from the applications. Therefore, bad implementations are hushed up. However, if software is implemented successfully it is typically discussed openly. Therefore, much like the floor of a casino (where the winning slots make a lot of noise and the losing slots are quiet) the positive observations are greatly over-estimated and over-emphasized.

6. Even if the reference company likes their present software, to what are they compared? This is explained well in an article on software selection. *"Before making a final decision, you should always check vendor references, but take them with a healthy grain of salt. An organization's satisfaction with software depends not only on how well it meets their needs, but how familiar they are with their options—there are a lot of people who are happy using difficult, labor-heavy, limited applications simply because they don't know there are better alternatives."—Idealware*

However, reference checks can be much better managed and much more useful than they generally are. Rather than asking if the company was happy with software XYZ, it can be more useful to ask how they are using software XYZ. This is much less judgmental and will tend to get to the bottom of how deeply the software is being used. The less judgmental the question, the more likely one is to get to the bottom of what really happened in a software implementation. It can also make sense to prepare a questionnaire that can be sent to the reference in advance. This questionnaire needs to be limited in the number of questions it has, because references cannot be expected to put a great deal of effort into answering these questions.

Conclusion

It should not be news to anyone that information that comes out of sales in any area is often not reliable. This of course also extends to marketing literature. However, there is also an enormous continuum of accuracy along which any vendor can reside. For instance, I have found that when a marketing message comes from SAP it will be either outright false, an exaggeration or a misrepresentation of the facts. Because of this, I have to verify the statement through my own research. However, on the other end of the continuum is the example of Arena Solutions, where I have yet to find something inaccurate in their marketing documentation. However, I can say these things with confidence about both of these software vendors because I have worked with these software vendors for years and read a very large amount of documentation by both companies and have firsthand experience with their applications. When one is new to a software vendor it makes sense to take a skeptical approach to their marketing documentation and statements.

When the topic turns to the software demo, there are all types of simple ways to improve the accuracy of information that is received from a demo that buyers do not take advantage of. The first principle on which the demo should be based is that the demo is entirely for the benefit of the buying company. This means that the buyer has the right to control the demo as they see fit, and to have his or her own people participate in using the application during the demo. Luckily this is an easy matter with modern web conferencing applications where various people can take control of the computers that are presenting. Demos have well-known limitations, the easiest to understand is that demos provide a small amount of time to the evaluators to actually get exposure to the application. Companies with the weakest applications have the greatest incentives to limit the buyer interaction with the application and have the software selection made on more strategic and abstract grounds. The converse is also true. The vendors with the best software want you to spend more time with their application. One example of this is Arena Solutions. Arena Solutions offers a 30 day free trial of their software, and is happy to sell a single license to a company for roughly $80 per month for one user. They know, that once in the door, their application has a high likelihood of being used, and for more users to ask their management for a license. Software vendors like SAP want a major commitment up front. Once the commitment is made, the buyer's flexibility is greatly limited. I have performed software recovery analysis for many companies for applications that never should have been purchased. However, after so much money has been spent on the software license, as well as the implementation, there is a very strong disincentive to move away from the sunk cost of a bad decision. This is actually a major difference between on-premises versus SaaS vendors. With SaaS vendors there is a much greater incentive to keep their customers satisfied, because a SaaS customer can more easily terminate their software subscription.

Integration is a major area of overemphasis in software selections. First, any application can be made to integrate with any other application, and many pre-built adapters that are marketed by software vendors are often much less than they appear during the sales process. Some software vendors, because of their desire to control the purchases of their clients toward their products have deliberately exaggerated the costs of application integration to clients. In fact, ERP purchases have been greatly justified by the desire to reduce integration costs.

However, as is explained in the SCM Focus Press book *The Real Story Behind ERP: Separating Fact from Fiction*, the percentage of integration costs that make up IT budgets has not declined after the introduction of ERP systems so the concept of ERP reducing integration costs has been all marketing hyperbole. The primary objective of any software selection should be to get the best application, which can meet the business requirements, not to attempt to save money, for which there is no evidence will be saved, by trying to minimize integration costs with other applications.

Client references sound like an easy way to find out information about how effective the software has been in other accounts. However, in practice client references are tricky. It would be more useful to actually speak to the system's users than the executives, but those resources are generally not made available during a client reference check. How to best manage reference checks to get more accurate information was explained in this chapter.

CHAPTER 7

How to Manage the Software Selection Process

This is the most conventional chapter in the book. While there are few books on software selection, there are some articles that focus on how to do the basic parts of software selection such as asking for responses from the vendors, and creating a vendor selection matrix. The reason I call these tasks "basic" is that literally anyone can do them, and for the most part they are not what differentiates successful software selections from the unsuccessful. As I stated in the book's introduction, the most important part of a software selection is not the elementary blocking and tackling, but the ***evaluation of the information that is brought into the software selection process.*** The almost total ignorance on this issue was a main motivation for writing this type of book in the first place. However, this book would be incomplete without a nod to these other undertakings, and in fact I have found that there are some ways to improve even these basic activities.

The Different Roles of the Software Selection Team

Michael Burns, in his article *Software Selection Done Right,* describes the software selection team in the following way:

> *"At our first meeting, we also explain the roles and responsibilities for the project. We typically identify roles for the sponsor, steering committee, project manager, project coordinator, business-process owners, subject-matter experts and technical leads. The idea is to determine which tasks fall within the purview of each role and to name the people responsible. It is essential that the right people be assigned to the project. For example, the project manager must be very organized and subject-matter experts must be highly knowledgeable about their business processes. Also, they must have enough time for the project."*

While I love the idea, I have never seen a software selection team so dutifully configured. In fact, I cannot even recall very much input being solicited from the business-process owners, subject matter experts or the technical leads. Most executives seem to think they have all the requisite knowledge to make the decision as long as they have seen a demo and read the Gartner Magic Quadrant Report on the software to be selected. I don't see how multiple areas of expertise could be leveraged (as proposed by a number of authors) into advice that is followed because I observe clients being blind-sided continually by requirements that cannot be met by the software they selected. Furthermore ***few people within the buyer have enough time to dedicate to the software selection***. However, this intelligent orientation regarding team development and providing employees with sufficient time to participate and contribute to the software selection is shown in the quotation below from the book *Modern ERP:*

> *"ERP system implementations require a significant human resource cost. Smart companies dedicate their most valuable and knowledgeable employees to the ERP project for a significant period of time. Each team member will need to educate other members on their respective functional area. Commitment to the team will undoubtedly conflict with the employees' normal job functions.... Creating the optimum team often requires backfilling key personnel to allow those chosen on the team to be fully dedicated to the implementation."*

Again, this also sounds great. But it just is not done in practice, or at least not frequently. Instead the participants are expected to fit the software selection in with their regular duties, but they are given very little incentive to make software selection a priority. Those on software selection teams are generally juggling their software selection duties on top of their regular work. This is one basic reason that software selections are performed so poorly. When I arrive at a client, I can find no well-reasoned explanation that has been documented as to why software was selected. If I am lucky I will be able to find a spreadsheet/matrix, which describes the different criteria that were selected. Companies simply do not make software selection a priority. Therefore, while Michael Burns is describing the right approach, I question how much time I should spend explaining the different roles if companies are unwilling to incorporate the input from such a large cross-section of the company. I found this comment from Michael Burns amusing:

> *"First, many of them know the business really well and can add a lot of value and input. Second, they are more likely to buy into the selection decision."*

This is absolutely true, but it is also generally true that input from these individuals is not valued. Does this attitude lead to bad decision-making? Yes, it does. However, I don't think this will change by me writing a book on the topic. We have entered a new era of elitism in the US where the executives know everything, add most of the value in the company, and the rest of the company is basically expected to "go with the flow." How often do we hear about the insights and experience of the top managers of the company, that must receive top compensation or else they will fly away to another company. Compare this to how often we hear about the insight of technologists or applications users and how important they are to the company's success. It's a question worth considering, because if we have a flawed model as to where the knowledge lies that is required to make good software selection decisions, poor decisions will continue to be made.

On the other hand, I only have consulted with large companies, and large companies tend to be quite hierarchical and therefore exclusionary. Also, as an implementer, I have not seen as many software selections as others. I know the job is not being done well, because I deal with the fall out. The individuals who see the most software selections are those who work in a sales or marketing capacity for a software vendor. For this reason I decided to ask a few colleagues their opinions of how well most software selections are performed. These individuals work in senior leadership roles in marketing in some vendors. I received some interesting responses.

> *"I have seen so many variations, with perhaps these common themes:*
>
> - *Processes that are too 'top down' and IT-driven just as you describe, especially in ERP and commodity buys.*
>
> - *Others where the 'users rule,' also not so good because they tend to block innovative thinking.*
>
> - *The best processes tend to be driven by line-of-business middle managers, who often are low enough to understand the subtleties of what they need, but high enough to be able to think outside the box. So for instance, in our area, a supply chain director.*
>
> *I would also say that procurement (i.e., software selection) processes have actually gotten marginally better in terms of 'due diligence' since the 'go-go' days you and I remember.[10] I can remember C-Level deals that weren't vetted at all.*
>
> *In supply chain, that rarely happens, and in fact the RFI process can become rather too long and laborious, with perhaps adding little value for the extensive level of effort required."*

The Role of the Coordinator

In a software selection, the decision makers will be a company's executive leadership, typically a combination of business and IT executives. Finance will be involved when it comes to discussions about budgets and money, but unless the application is finance-related (that is, software for their department), they are typically not that involved in the software selection process. However, while executives are the primary decision makers, they do not necessarily have to be the ones managing the process.

---

[10] Here he is referring to the technology boom of the late 1990s.

One weakness of many software selection initiatives is that the executives often try to manage all of the logistics of the process, when in fact it makes much more sense to assign the task to a manager-level individual in the company. As long as this person is not overwhelmed with other work (something to be considered when making the assignment), he or she provides a significant benefit in managing logistics and communication, in maintaining the folder of vendor documentation and the requirements list, and in tabulating the scores for the vendors. They may also have domain expertise if they are chosen from the area where the software is to be implemented. These are the major roles of the software selection coordinator:

1. *Manage the Communication with all of the vendors:* This includes everything from the initial introduction, to providing feedback on what the buyer would like to see demonstrated and how they would like the demonstration to be presented.

2. *Timing administration:* Setting up the meetings and managing the calendar and logistics for web meetings and for vendor visits to the buyer's site.

3. *Maintain the network folders for the implementation:* These folders include correspondence from the vendors, their marketing literature, screen shots, IT analyst reports; anything that is pertinent to the software selection should be maintained in such a way that all the decision makers can easily find it and review it at their convenience.

4. *Development of the Vendor Grading Document:* This means continually updating the document with contextual information as well as maintaining the scores.

5. *Serving as a mediator for all meetings:* This ranges from managing introductions to walking the executives through the vendor grading document.

Having a single person do this increases the likelihood that the things that need to get done will get done in a consistent manner. The executives themselves decide how much of a vote they would like the coordinator to have in the final software selection. As the coordinator should be from the area where the software is to be implemented, he or she should be able to offer good, detailed advice to the executives.

Beyond domain expertise, the coordinator should have the following qualities:

1. *They should have the respect of the executives:* Part of the coordinator's role is to serve as a moderator, and this means managing the interaction of the executives. This is related particularly to the next topic.

2. *They should mediate selection bias:* Software selection is frequently victim to selection bias. This means that each executive decision maker will seek to find the best software for the group or department that he or she represents, rather than the software that offers the best overall compromise for the company. This issue is most prevalent on ERP projects because ERP applications are such a diverse combination of functionalities. Applications that are more narrow in focus are less affected by this bias, but the problem arises again when buyers purchase software suites from one vendor rather than software from separate vendors for each category.

3. *They must be organized and good at documentation:* This will be necessary to perform the coordination and maintain the documentation.

4. *They must be good communicators:* The coordinator will need to communicate with many individuals and so must be able to do so in an efficient manner.

Implementing the Scientific Method in the Software Selection

In the introduction to this book I explained that the advice provided would focus on making the software selection process more scientific. Many people confuse science with sophisticated technology or scientific instruments. However, to be scientific is simply to follow principles related to how testing is performed. Following the scientific method does not require any scientific knowledge or even fancy equipment. This is explained in the quotation below from Wikipedia on the scientific method:

> *"Scientific inquiry is generally intended to be as objective as possible in order to reduce biased interpretations of results. Another basic expectation is to document, archive and share all data and methodology so they are available for careful scrutiny by other scientists, giving them the opportunity to verify results by attempting to reproduce them. This practice, called full disclosure, also allows*

*statistical measures of the reliability of these data to be established
(when data is sampled or compared to chance)."*

The analogy between software selection and science is, of course, not perfect. A company does not actually publish the results of its software selection documentation for other companies to evaluate and reproduce. Unlike public entities, private companies don't have any interest in helping other people understand what they are doing or in advancing knowledge. Instead their objective is to "maximize shareholder value," which essentially means to maximize the share price. In fact, even public companies do not publish the software selection results.[11] However, portions of the software selection can be approached scientifically and the following sections will explain how.

The Importance of Documentation in the Software Selection Process

Gregor Mendel is an excellent example of the importance of documenting observations. He advanced the understanding of genetics through the rather low-tech approach of measuring the characteristics of successive generations of peas, which he grew in the garden of his monastery.[12]

> *"By simply counting peas and keeping meticulous notes, Mendel
> established the principles of inheritance, coined the terms dominant
> and recessive, and was the first to use statistical methods to
> analyze and predict hereditary information. For eight years, Mendel
> cultivated thousands of pea plants and used a paintbrush to
> painstakingly transfer pollen from one plant to another to make his
> crosses (all the while still attending to his duties as a monk and a
> teacher)."* — Wikipedia

His research paper is still available, at a link that is in the reference section of this book. His notes are quite meticulous, and this was a researcher who really knew how to document his results. With Mendel's disciplined and scientific mind,

---

[11] I certainly knew it was not common for companies or the government to publish the results of software selection; however I decided to search to see if I could find published results of this type and I was not able to find any examples.

[12] Mendel was an Augustinian friar, but was also a professor of physics.

he would have been excellent at software selection, or any area, which required a detailed and analytical mind.

Science works because it follows a set of rules that allows for objective comparison of the variables to be observed. Documentation is a big part of the scientific approach because our memories are far from perfect, and recording allows for comparisons across observations that are separated in time. For example, not all the vendors that a buyer is looking at will present their demos on the same day. Information from vendors and from other sources will similarly be time lagged. Secondly, information will come to different people. Consistently documenting these disparate data points allows them to be analyzed in a controlled manner. It also allows others to analyze them in a comprehensive fashion both prior to the software selection decision as well as after the fact. There is a list of what is called cognitive biases (such as confirmation bias, which is the predisposition to search for data points that support pre-existing beliefs) and many of these cognitive biases are at least partially addressed through thorough documentation.

Tabulating the Scores for Each Vendor

Some software selections use a formalized scoring spreadsheet and some do not. Some companies simply write a short report for why the software was selected, but many do not. However, for the following reasons I would very much recommend putting together some type of scoring sheet:

1. Software selection means comparing a large number of criteria. It is difficult to really see how the vendor products compare across so many criteria without some type of graphical representation.

2. The scoring document clearly communicates to everyone what criteria are being used for the selection and how the software under consideration is weighted. I am surprised to see so many software selection spreadsheets that do not have the ability to weight the criteria. The executives do not have to agree on the weighting. Each can provide a weight, which can be adjusted based upon how much of a vote they have. However, the company needs to come to an agreement on the weight per criteria.

3. At the final selection meeting, having a document helps ground the discussion and allows everyone to use a single frame of reference for the decision.

Many of the executives will have missed some of the data that has been documented in the scoring spreadsheet. Reviewing the scoring document will help bring all the executives, as well as other software selection team members, to the same understanding.

4. A software selection is an important decision for the company. For such a decision it's important that the outcome is based upon as much objectivity as possible. I find that matrix helps increase objectivity.

5. The scoring document becomes a long-term reference for the company. It is also useful for the stage that follows software selection: negotiation (covered in the following paragraphs).

6. The software selection matrix is easy to do.

I have placed a sample software selection matrix below.

Software Selection Comparison Matrix

Criteria Columns		Solutions Compared Columns			Weight Per Criteria
Criteria	Category of Criteria	Vendor 1	Vendor 2	Vendor 3	
Value to the Business - ROI Potential	Business	5	10	7	4
Total Cost of Ownership (higher score means lower value)	Project	3	4	5	4
References	Software	3	8	9	2
The Ability to Compare Costs of Goods vs. Transportation Costs	Software	6	6	4	1
Effort required to migrate current customized solution to the new solution	Project	3	7	8	1
Incorporation of Warehouse Space Savings	Software	5	5	6	1
Service Level Improvement Potential	Software	4	10	8	2
Transparency of the Solution	Business	5	9	7	2
The Ability to Schedule at Will	Business	5	8	4	1
Allow Flexibility in Exclusions	Business	7	6	2	1
Weighed Scores		**82**	**84**	**76**	

A software selection matrix combines the scores for each vendor for a variety of criteria along with the criteria weight. This software selection matrix is simply one example, and of course it can be extended to have any number of criteria. The individuals who are part of the selection must agree as to the weight per criteria. As soon as that is done, the vendors are rate, and oftentimes sorted on the basis of their combined score.

I have used a derivation of this matrix and I have always found it useful. Occasionally individuals who are pulling for a particular vendor will criticize the scoring document by saying something like, "*I already know what the scoring will be, so I don't have to look at it.*" Typically these statements are an attempt to undermine a rational approach to the software selection and to minimize the inputs of others so that their preferred vendor can win. Emotions can run high during a software selection, which is why it's important to gain agreement on both the criteria and the weight assigned to each criterion (which can be voted on, resulting in a blended weight) **before** the software is scored.

The criteria and weights should be reviewed several times and then set in stone. If the weights are reviewed or requests to change the weights are received after the software vendor gets its rating, then what is most likely happening is that the data is being changed to fit a desired outcome. The methodology of the scoring for the software selection should be straightforward. The winning vendor should be the one with the highest combined weight output of all the criteria. Anything can be included as criteria—price, the perceived ease of working with the vendor—the criteria are subjective. They are whatever the software selection team chooses to value.

There are competing ideas regarding the inclusion of vendors that the buyer cannot afford. On one hand, the buyer is wasting the vendor's time and their own time. On the other hand the company learns more about what is available in the marketplace as well as understanding what they are trading off to get a vendor they can afford. There is no perfect answer to this question.

Making the Decision

There has been a good deal of research into group decision-making. One of the findings is that the more vocal members of a group easily influence other group members, even if the more vocal members do not necessarily have more domain expertise than the less vocal members. What is desirable is that each individual makes their own decision such that the decision is reached independently and is *not unduly influenced by the personality of one or a few people.* To accomplish this outcome, the RAND Corporation developed the Delphi Method, named after the city of Delphi in Greece, the location of the Oracles who were consulted by the Ancient Greeks and Romans, among many others. RAND's research into the Delphi Method goes back to 1943 when they performed a number of studies on this topic. The original intent of the research was to obtain better group judgment, by performing research, for example, into how the effect of strong personality types on groups can be mitigated (the research isolated the participants from one another). The Delphi Method eliminates the group interaction as explained by RAND:

> *"RAND developed the Delphi method in the 1950s, originally to forecast the impact of technology on warfare. The method entails a group of experts who anonymously reply to questionnaires and subsequently receive feedback in the form of a statistical representation of the 'group response,' after which the process repeats itself. The goal is to reduce the range of responses and arrive at something closer to expert consensus. The Delphi Method has been widely adopted and is still in use today."* — RAND

The Delphi Method is often thought to relate directly to forecasting only, and in fact is an approach to consensus-based forecasting. However, it applies to any decision-making situation. The research into consensus decision-making, much of which was rolled into the Delphi Method, is useful for software selection, as is shown in the following quote about the Delphi Method (the emphasis is mine):

> *"The Delphi method (/ˈdɛlfaɪ/ del-fy) is a structured communication technique, originally developed as a systematic, interactive forecasting method which relies on a panel of experts. The experts answer questionnaires in two or more rounds. After each round, a facilitator provides an anonymous summary of the experts' forecasts from the previous round as well as the reasons they provided for their judgments. Thus, experts are encouraged to revise their earlier answers in light of the replies of other members of their panel. It is believed that during this process the range of the answers will*

*decrease and the group will converge towards the 'correct' answer. Finally, the process is stopped after a predefined stop criterion (e.g., number of rounds, achievement of consensus, stability of results) and the mean or median scores of the final rounds determine the results. Delphi is based on the principle that forecasts (or decisions) from a **structured group of individuals are more accurate than those from unstructured groups.**"* —Wikipedia

Interestingly, I have never heard of an approach to making the software selection process more scientific and less susceptible to the influence of one or a few individuals. I also very much doubt that executives at a company would agree to something like the Delphi Method, as getting together with other executives is the normal way that decisions are made in most companies. On the other hand, people that reviewed this book prior to its publication have told me that they did something similar in their software selection, even though they may not have related it to the Delphi Method. One quotation I have included below:

"I facilitated two software selections. As I recall our methodology was to form a team comprised of middle management from the user department and IT, and we reported to upper management. We 'workshopped' the vendor questionnaire. I facilitated the workshops in a participatory manner that honoured all input without (too much) judgment and arrived at a consensus on the questionnaire. The questionnaire was based on the current business process (with improvements that could be taken advantage of if new software was acquired) and on user requirements in addition to IT's requirements. So, in this case executives did agree to both the consensus process (probably because they didn't care how it got done, just that it got done) and to the decision that was made via the process. We continued the consensus all the way through to selection without much dispute, and the same team, more or less, worked on the implementation. Because there was firm agreement on the criteria and on the software selected, we knew exactly what we were getting into and the implementation was very smooth."

However, as I have explained with numerous examples, the current approach to software selection results in poor outcomes. The current design means that vendor sales and marketing count for more than the actual software. Companies that follow the realistic approach as outlined in this book can greatly improve the outcomes of the software they select.

Moving from Selection to Vendor Negotiations

As I do not have experience in negotiating with software vendors, I am not qualified to advise on the topic of vendor negotiations. Furthermore, a different group than the team that performed the software selection typically handles this part of the process. But the software selection is an input to the negotiation process, and the thoroughness of the software selection process can put those that negotiate with the vendors in the best possible position. Here is how:

1. Often the group that performs the software negotiation, which may be from the procurement or contracts department, will not be familiar with the software and will not have participated in the software selection process. Therefore, it's important to have an easy-to-understand document that explains the conclusions of the software selection.

2. The vendor negotiation group should keep in contact with the software selection coordinator. There are all types of reasons for this, but one is so that the negotiation group does not lose the context of the software selection. Secondly, there were statements made by the vendor during the software selection, and those statements should not "go away" when the contract is about to be signed. A frequent technique is to sell one thing, but then have the contract say something that is more modest. Some very experienced consultants recommend writing the important promises from the sales process into the contract. By keeping a good communication level between the software selection coordinator and the vendor negotiation group, the buyer can stay out of these traps. Finally, the coordinator, and possibly other members of the software selection team need to review the software license and consulting agreement before it is signed. This will be a tedious process because much of the documentation will be in legalese. Rather than having each person try to get through the contracts themselves, it can make more

sense to go through the documents as a group, and to have the company's internal council there to translate what things mean in plain English.

3. The software selection process will result in a list of vendors, which can be sorted from the first choice to the remaining choices. As with any purchase decision, the first choice may lose out to the second or third choice when negotiations determine that an agreeable arrangement cannot be arrived at with the first choice. A thoroughly-filled out software selection scoring matrix explains not only the sequence of the choices, but also the degree of preference for one vendor over another. This gives very important information to the individual/group negotiating with the software vendor. A small differential between the top-rated vendors means that the negotiating group can look for opportunities for a lower price from another vendor to tip the balance in their favor. For instance, in the sample-scoring matrix shown previously, there is a very small difference between Vendor 1 and Vendor 2, and only a one-point difference between the estimated total cost of ownership (TCO). If Vendor 2, the top choice, were to take a hard position in the negotiation, Vendor 1 would seem to be an available option for this buyer.

4. The software selection team should be careful to communicate the TCO aspect of the selection (which is a criterion in my software selection matrix), because without this context the negotiating team may be blind to these costs and make their negotiating decision based upon the initial purchase price only. This will require the software selection team to have made certain assumptions regarding the total cost of ownership. It's not an easy task, as TCO is tricky and has many factors, which must be added to the calculation. I believe it is more realistic, given the resources that companies seem willing to allocate to software selection projects, to simply rate a vendor's predicted TCO on a scale from one to ten. The TCO value can be either added to the scoring matrix or assigned a weight. However, a thorough software selection would result in an estimate. The topic of TCO as well as self-service estimation is covered at our companion site, Software Decisions.[13]

There is also a question of whether to exclude those vendors entirely when it is suspected that their price will be too high. However, vendors are cagey regarding

---

[13] The Software Decisions website is available at http://www.softwaredecisions.org

the price of their software and it can depend upon many factors, including which other products produced by the vendor the buyer currently owns. Furthermore, the "real price" can drop different degrees per vendor per situation, depending upon how the negotiation proceeds. This, of course, greatly increases the complexity of the selection process and reduces the transparency and efficiency of the enterprise software market.

Conclusion

Most publications on software selection cover the tactical elements of software selection far better than the broader or interpretational elements. This book has taken the opposite approach, focusing on how to interpret information that is received from the multiple sources that influence software selection. I allocated much less space to the tactical elements of software selection. However, this chapter covered these tactical elements of how to manage the software selection process.

The software selection coordinator role is quite important to the effectiveness of the overall software selection process. In this chapter, I laid out the characteristics that make a good coordinator. It's relatively easy to begin a software selection process without a coordinator, however, this is misleading. As the software selection proceeds there is more coordination required, more items that must be followed up, and eventually the requirement for a mediator between all the members of the software selection team. The coordinator should have the most time allocated to the software selection project of any of the team members (and needs to have this reflected in the rest of their workload) and should be able to keep the team focused, as well as provide the team with the necessary context to both interpret information and explain to them accurately how the software selection has proceeded up until the current discussion. A coordinator can allocate the type of time to a software selection that such an initiative requires, and the type of time commitment that the executives often cannot make.

Software selections can be greatly improved by increasing the use of the scientific method, which is a structured approach to the testing of any hypothesis. Science works because it follows a set of rules that allows for objective comparison of the variables to be observed. And a big part of this process is to document information that is uncovered during the software selection. This documentation helps increase the rationality of the overall process and can help to place on even footing information that is often gathered months apart. A software selection matrix, which is a condensed way of making these comparisons, is not uncommon, but documentation during the software selection process should not be limited simply to comparison spreadsheets of this type. Documents with detailed explanations of the rationale for the positives and negatives of the various compared applications should also be created and made available to the current software selection team members as well as archived for future software selections. Documentation, and reviewing this documentation, can have the positive effect of mitigating the natural tendency of one or a few individuals with strong personalities and strong opinions from imposing their selection on the rest of the team. For instance, while a person may have only one vote in terms of their official capacity on the selection team, through the force of their personality, and their ability to persuade, they may be able to coopt other members to essentially give up their vote to these individuals. The excessive influence of some individuals on group decision-making is why the RAND Corporation developed the Delphi Method. The Delphi Method makes the "voting" private, which tends to be less influenced by factors such as being in the same room with an influential individual. This is also why political voting is performed behind a curtain of some type.

Once the software selection has been made, typically the negotiation of the contract is transitioned to another group. This is where the documentation that was developed during the software selection can be put to another good use by allowing the group that performs negotiation to understand why the vendor was selected. The group that negotiates must know not only the first choice, but the second and even third choice because an agreeable arrangement may not be feasible between the buyer and the first choice. A thoroughly-filled out software selection scoring matrix explains not only the sequence of the choices, but also the degree of preference for one vendor over another. However, someone who was part of the software selection team should keep in contact with the group that performs the negotiation. There are some with expertise in this area that believe that a person from the software selection team is in the best position to perform the negotiation with the software vendor, however, this is both often not feasible because of how companies are structured, but I question if this is the right approach because negotiation is really a different skill than software selection. If I take myself as an example, while I am qualified to perform any supply chain planning application software selection I do not negotiate contracts and would be at a distinct disadvantage performing the negotiation against a software vendor as they would certainly have a professional negotiator. I would think the best possible combination would be for the member of the software selection team to work with the individual with negotiating expertise in order to perform the negotiation together. Furthermore, the software selection team should be careful to communicate the TCO aspect of the selection (which is a criterion in my software selection matrix that I showed in this chapter), because without this context the negotiating team may be blind to these costs and make their negotiating decision based upon the initial purchase price only.

CHAPTER 8

Conclusion

In order to improve software selection outcomes, one must understand the incentives of all the parties involved in providing information to buyers. This includes, vendors, consulting companies, IT analyst firms, and publications. That is, the first step to analyzing the information provided by various entities is to analyze the entities themselves. Once time is spent analyzing each of these entities, clear patterns emerge that can allow the buyer to separate the true from the untrue. Not enough companies do this, and it is one reason that software selections at companies result too often in the wrong software being selected. I have found extensive evidence for this fact in my own consulting experience—when I am hired to help recover problematic supply chain planning implementations. However, that is, of course, anecdotal and related to a particular software area, but research supports the fact that this conclusion generalizes to other software areas. For example, in the SCM Focus Press book *The Real Story Behind ERP: Separating Fact from Fiction*, is a review of the research into the long term benefits of ERP software. The book explains that the studies on ERP software show that ERP is a software category with a low return on investment. However, there is a missing component to all of the research in this area. ERP can maintain a low return on investment only if one limits the financial returns to the ERP system itself. However, it is quite likely that ERP systems have a negative ROI when one accounts for how ERP negatively impacts the overall software investment by a company (for instance if the negative effect on other applications the company uses, as well as how ERP isolates companies from customers and suppliers, are included in the calculation).[14] Nonetheless, ERP has been the most popularly purchased software in the enterprise software market for decades. Buying companies have fallen for the most oversimplified fictions presented by ERP vendors and consulting companies, which are hungry for the ERP implementation budget. The fact that such statements related to the purchase of ERP, which had never had any evidence to support them, bamboozled so many companies is some of the best evidence that I can provide that buying companies are simply not doing sufficient research before making purchases. The areas where buyers are falling down in their research are the following:

1. My consulting experience provides evidence (although not conclusive evidence as there are not enough companies in the sample) that companies choose the wrong software far too frequently within a particular software category (i.e., if within one category of software, vendor A offers the best product and fit for the company, too often the company will select vendor B).

2. My research into the benefits of ERP indicates that companies are not performing broader research into the benefits of entire categories of software that they purchase. Instead they are accepting the proposals of entities that are trying to sell them things, and that also do not perform research on the actual benefits of various software categories.

Buying companies **must** perform this type of research themselves. They simply cannot realistically "outsource" this research to IT analysts because too many

---

[14] For those that are skeptical of this, I would expect skepticism. ERP is, of course, extremely popular software, how can it be ineffective? The totality of the explanation of why ERP has never been shown to provide the benefits it promised cannot be fully explained in a few paragraphs, which is why I wrote an entire book on the topic that addresses this issue in detail. I have worked with ERP systems for sixteen years before I wrote this book, and I was surprised myself by what I found. All I knew on my ERP projects was that something was "amiss," but could not put my finger on it. I consider this story to be the most surprising I have ever covered in enterprise software. This intent of explaining the issues with ERP is to simply show that what I have found through direct experience is clearly not merely limited to the area of software in which I specialize.

IT analysts (Gartner, Forrester, etc.) are paid by vendors. These IT analysts can write articles about how to "improve" the use or implementation of a category of software, but cannot write an article questioning the entire validity of a software category or even mildly questioning *the return on investment of a category of software without alienating the losing revenues from those vendors.* Most of these IT analyst firms have continual revenue growth targets, and material or opinions that interfere with those revenue targets will not be tolerated.

While those in marketing will disagree, software cannot be optimized for both sales and implement-ability. Software that is highly implementable means that product management has accounted for the important enhancements but has not put every enhancement request into the product. A major objective of the individuals who support a software selection effort is to ignore much of the marketing hyperbole and salesmanship and instead find the applications that offer the best combination of functionality to match with the buyer's requirements, while at the same time considering the implement-ability of that functionality.

Consulting companies are major influencers for enterprise software purchasing decisions. Both institutional analysis as well as my consulting experience support the fact that large consulting companies, as well as most of the smaller consulting companies, are making selection advice based upon their own revenue goals and that their client's interests do not factor into the advice they provide. A consulting company can make a smaller amount of money providing objective advice in software selection, but far more money if they pretend to sell objective advice and use it as a doorway into the much more lucrative implementation deal. As we all know, the "responsibility" of companies is to maximize shareholder value, so that is what these companies are doing. This is an excellent way to achieve that objective.

IT analyst firms, with Gartner being the most prominent, are influential in which software gets purchased. Gartner sells "research." However, the research is not only difficult to interpret, it is deliberately opaque because Gartner is trying to have it both ways. They want to rate software (and hardware and service) vendors, but also make their money from these vendors, so have chosen an approach to publishing that requires interpretation—and this interpretation is provided by them at great expense through hiring their analysts for one-on-one sessions. Gartner's research can be corrected by adjusting downward the rankings for the larger vendors as they are inflated, and this is just one of the adjustments that are necessary. Gartner's research can be leveraged, but the way it is normally used makes me question whether a Gartner subscription does more harm than good. I am particularly concerned with the use of Gartner and their Magic Quadrant as a device for enforcing conformity, simply mindlessly selecting software that ranks well in the Magic Quadrant without even understanding Gartner's methodology. Executives that use Gartner to simply cover themselves politically, and do very little research on their own, or leverage their own internal technical resources, are weak executives and are not doing their job.

For those embarking on a new software selection, the good news is that there are many opportunities to improve your software selection by simply following the recommendations in this book. There is very little training on software selection, and little in the way of published material that is not simply focused on the tactical areas of software selection. The starting point is not the tactics, but is in how information is interpreted. This must be understood first, even before the other very important parts of software selection are discussed.

There is a lot of great software available in the enterprise software market. I find myself bowled over by some of the great innovation in a number of vendors that I follow. They keep me on my toes and provide a constant stream of interesting topics on which to write articles and books. A good software selection project can bring that software into the company. On the other hand, there is also quite a lot of completely uninspired software that is extremely unappealing to work with (some of the same software I specialize in, in fact!) and is clearly sold because not enough people can see the distinctions in software quality or because other non-application related factors dominate the software selection decision. Good software, which has been properly selected, brings continuous returns and implements more easily because it is both appealing to use and it naturally works and fits with the business requirements. There is an enormous amount of intellectual property tied up in our enterprise software. From 1970, where the software industry essentially did not exist, up until when I write this sentence, software has grown in capabilities to an enormous extent. In my area, some of the most advanced mathematics in my field are encapsulated in software. It is the only way through which companies could ever access and apply such intelligence. However, the trick, of course, is making the right selection.

How to Use Independent Consultants for Software Selection

One of the biggest mistakes made by executive decision-makers is that more often than not they go into interactions with software vendors without technical resources to advise them. While some executive decision-makers may have worked in software previously, it is not the executive's role, at least in US corporations, to be up on technology. Decisions regarding information technology purchases are most often made by a combination of IT and the business that will use the application (for instance the finance department for financial software). However, being a bit distant from the technology is not only common with the executives from business departments, but is also true even of executive decision-makers who work in IT, such as the CIO and Vice Presidents. At that level, the work is much more abstract, focused more on budgets and on making the numbers work than on technology. However, when software vendors make a number of technology contentions during demos or when providing information during interactions with the executives within the prospect company, the executives are not in the best position to verify this information. Furthermore, as the prospective buyer does not own the software, technical resources internal to the company are not in the best position to verify the claims made by the software vendors. Relying upon a consulting company typically will not provide the necessary information due to the bias of consulting firms that was described in Chapter 4: "How to Use Consulting Advice on Software Selection."

The best-case scenario here is to find an independent consultant through something like LinkedIn. Independent consultants who have experience in the application can be hired and can verify statements made by the software vendor. However, a few rules should be followed to ensure that you control for bias as much as possible.

1. When the independent consultant is hired, it should be made clear that the consultant will only participate in the software selection phase. If the independent consultant believes that he or she may gain more work after the selection, it will bias the independent consultant most likely in favor of the software vendor—so that he or she can then work on the implementation.

2. When searching for an independent consultant, it's important to find one that has exposure to several applications in the area so that they can compare and contrast for you the different applications. During software selection, multiple companies present to the prospect, and the independent consultant that you choose should be familiar with several of these applications.

3. During the interview with the independent consultant, determine if the consultant can see the positives and negatives to the applications that he or she will be helping you evaluate. If the consultant is simply a cheerleader for one application, then he or she will not be able to help you, even if quite knowledgeable in the technology.

4. Independent consultants move from project to project. Software selection projects, because they are shorter, are not as desirable to consultants as implementation projects, which are much longer contracts. You cannot expect an independent consultant to be available exactly when you want to review software vendors. However, you can hire independent consultants part time and remotely. That means they educate you remotely, listen in through a conference call, view the demo through a web conference, and review the material given to you remotely. This remote approach is quite a bit more cost effective and most independent consultants would be amenable

to this arrangement. On the other hand, if the independent consultant is available to work full time, there are advantages in that the consultant can provide a general education about the software category and can help with structuring the analysis for the software selection. In many cases, executive decision-makers are busy attending meetings or with other operational tasks, and employing someone who can really concentrate on the software selection can provide benefits.

Of course, the problem arises when no independent consultant can be found who has experience in the particular software that is part of the selection. This is the case with smaller applications where the independent consulting market is simply not well developed. In this case, the best that can be done is to find an independent consultant with similar experience and exposure.

Conclusion

Executive decision-makers undermine the software selection process when they attempt to validate the statements and capabilities of applications in which neither they nor other people whose expertise they can draw upon, have experience with the applications being evaluated. The executive decision-maker is put into a position of weakness, making it difficult for the executive to make informed decisions. First-hand experience regarding all enterprise software is available and can be found on LinkedIn or Dice. Depending upon the circumstance and the availability of the desired independent consultant, he or she may be hired full time and work on site, or be hired to work remotely. An independent consultant is a far more reliable guide for advising on a software selection than a consulting company. Unlike the consulting company, an independent consultant is not attempting to staff consultants on the project. However, in order to minimize bias, it should also be explained to the independent consultant that they will not be part of the implementation in any way. This removes any financial bias of the independent consultant, making the consultant indifferent as to which software the company decides to implement. However, most companies lack this internal analytical capability, and end up making poor and expensive mistakes in software selection because of this. What is desperately needed in the marketplace is specialized entities that will provide corporate software buyers with the straight story and quality information on vendors, and that provide their advice within a historical context (this historical context is important, because if we simply talk about the future, anything can seem possible, however compared to history what is likely comes into focus). However, everywhere companies look when in need of advice on software selection, for the most part, find that the companies offering advice are only looking out for their own interests.

Other Books from SCM Focus

Bill of Materials in Excel, ERP, Planning and PLM/BMMS Software

http://www.scmfocus.com/scmfocuspress/the-software-approaches-for-improving-your-bill-of-materials-book/

Constrained Supply and Production Planning with SAP APO

http://www.scmfocus.com/scmfocuspress/select-a-book/constrained-supply-and-production-planning-in-sap-apo/

Enterprise Software Risk: Controlling the Main Risk Factors on IT Projects

http://www.scmfocus.com/scmfocuspress/it-decision-making-books/enterprise-software-project-risk-management/

Enterprise Software Selection: How to Pinpoint the Perfect Software Solution using Multiple Information Sources

http://www.scmfocus.com/scmfocuspress/it-decision-making-books/enterprise-software-selection/

Enterprise Software TCO: Calculating and Using Total Cost of Ownership for Decision Making

http://www.scmfocus.com/scmfocuspress/it-decision-making-books/enterprise-software-tco/

Gartner and the Magic Quadrant: A Guide for Buyers, Vendors, Investors

http://www.scmfocus.com/scmfocuspress/it-decision-making-books/gartner-and-the-magic-quadrant/

Inventory Optimization and Multi-Echelon Planning Software

http://www.scmfocus.com/scmfocuspress/supply-books/the-inventory-optimization-and-multi-echelon-software-book/

Multi Method Supply Planning in SAP APO

http://www.scmfocus.com/scmfocuspress/select-a-book/multi-method-supply-planning-in-sap-apo/

Planning Horizons, Calendars and Timings in SAP APO

http://www.scmfocus.com/scmfocuspress/select-a-book/planning-horizons-calendars-and-timings-in-sap-apo/

Process Industry Planning Software: Manufacturing Processes and Software

http://www.scmfocus.com/scmfocuspress/production-books/process-industry-planning/

Replacing Big ERP: Breaking the Big ERP Habit with Best of Breed Applications at a Fraction of the Cost

http://www.scmfocus.com/scmfocuspress/erp-books/replacing-erp/

Setting up the Supply Network in SAP APO

http://www.scmfocus.com/scmfocuspress/select-a-book/setting-up-the-supply-network-in-sap-apo/

SuperPlant: Creating a Nimble Manufacturing Enterprise with Adaptive Planning

http://www.scmfocus.com/scmfocuspress/production-books/the-superplant-concept/

Supply Chain Forecasting Software

http://www.scmfocus.com/scmfocuspress/the-statistical-and-consensus-supply-chain-forecasting-software-book/

Supply Planning with MRP/DRP and APS Software

http://www.scmfocus.com/scmfocuspress/supply-books/the-supply-planning-with-mrpdrp-and-aps-software-book/

The Real Story Behind ERP: Separating Fact from Fiction

http://www.scmfocus.com/scmfocuspress/erp-books/the-real-story-behind-erp/

Spreading the Word

SCM Focus Press is a small publisher. However, we pride ourselves on publishing the unvarnished truth, which most other publishers will not publish. If you felt like you learned something valuable from reading this book, please spread the word by adding a review on Amazon.com

Links in the Book

Chapter 1

http://www.scmfocus.com/writing-rules/

http://www.scmfocus.com

Chapter 2

http://www.scmfocus.com/enterprisesoftwarepolicy

Chapter 3

http://www.scmfocus.com/demandplanning/2010/09/why-companies-are-selecting-the-wrong-supply-chain-demand-planning-systems/

Chapter 4

http://www.scmfocus.com/productionplanningandscheduling/2012/11/16/a-review-of-plan4demands-ppds-webinar/

Chapter 5

http://www.scmfocus.com/enterprisesoftwarepolicy/2012/03/11/why-the-largest-enterprise-software-companies-have-no-reason-to-innovate/

http://www.scmfocus.com/scmhistory/2010/07/how-analysts-got-everything-wrong-on-marketplaces/

Chapter 6

http://vimeo.com/14844814

http://blip.tv/scm-focus/google-search-for-misuse-of-inventory-optimization-4122062

http://www.scmfocus.com/inventoryoptimizationmultiechelon/2010/01/its-time-for-the-sap-xapps-program-to-die/

http://www.scmfocus.com/sapprojectmanagement/2012/01/the-end-of-sap-solution-manager/

http://www.scmfocus.com/sapintegration/2011/11/15/what-are-saps-vendor-integration-certifications-worth-on-projects/

References

Arena Solutions. *BOM Control.* http://www.arenasolutions.com/products/
bomcontrol/features/item-management/
http://www.rand.org/standards.html

Bandor, Michael S. *Quantitative Methods for Software Selection and
Evaluation.* Carnegie Mellon University, 2006.

Bittman, Tom. *A Rant—My Integrity as an Analyst.* October 8, 2009.
http://blogs.gartner.com/
thomas_bittman/2009/10/08/a-rant-my-integrity-as-an-analyst/.

Blodget, Henry. *Moody's Analyst Breaks Silence.*
August 19, 2011. http://www.businessinsider.com/
moodys-analyst-conflicts-corruption-and-greed-2011-8?op=1.

Bradford, Marianne. *Modern ERP: Select, Implement and Use Today's
Advanced Business Systems.* Lulu, 2010.

Burns, Michael. *System selection, done right—Part I.* CA Magazine:
January-February 2012. http://www.camagazine.com/archives/print-
edition/2012/january-february/columns/camagazine54716.aspx.

Byrne, Tom. *Getting beyond the Magic Quadrant for WCM.*
August 26, 2010. http://www.realstorygroup.com/
Blog/1981-Getting-beyond-the-Magic-Quadrant-for-WCM.

Cameron, Preston D. *The Software Selection Questionnaire.* Phoenix
Publishing Group, 2002.

Campbell, Peter. The Perfect Fit: A Guide to Evaluating and Purchasing Major Software Systems. September, 2008. http://idealware.org/articles/purchasing_major_systems.php.

Columbus, Louis. *Gartner's Magic Quadrant May Need New Pixie Dust.* eCommerce Times: April 15, 2005. http://www.ecommercetimes.com/story/42302.html?wlc=1222636414.

Consumer Reports. *No Consumer Use Policy.* http://www.consumerreports.org/cro/about-us/no-commerical-use-policy/index.htm.

Consumer Reports. *Our Mission.* http://www.consumerreports.org/cro/about-us/our-mission/index.htm.

Delphi Method. Last modified July 9, 2013. http://en.wikipedia.org/wiki/Delphi_method.

Delphi Method. http://www.rand.org/topics/delphi-method.html.

Dilger, Daniel Eran. *Three years ago Gartner predicted Apple would go nowhere in smartphones.* October 21, 2012. http://www.roughlydrafted.com/2012/10/21/three-years-ago-gartner-predicted-apple-would-go-nowhere-in-smartphones/.

Ellman, Matthew and Germano, Fabrizio. *What do the papers sell? A model of advertising and media bias.* March 2008. https://docs.google.com/viewer?url=http%3A%2F%2Fwww.iae.csic.es%2FinvestigatorsMaterial%2Fa8287092114archivoPdf1062.pdf.

English, Larry. *How Best-of-breed Software Section Causes IQ Problems.* Information Management: October 1, 2003. http://www.information-management.com/issues/20031001/7434-1.html.

ERP system selection methodology. Last modified April 10, 2013. http://en.wikipedia.org/wiki/ERP_system_selection_methodology.

Francica, Joe. *Why Gartner's Magic Quadrant Missed the Importance of Location Analytics to Business Intelligence.* Last modified May 13, 2013. http://www.directionsmag.com/articles/why-gartners-magic-quadrant-missed-the-importance-of-location-analytic/326188.

Gartner Annual Report 2012
http://investor.gartner.com/phoenix.zhtml?c=99568&p=irol-reportsAnnual
http://www.linkedin.com/groups/
Gartners-Magic-Quadrant-Is-It-51825.S.149671061
http://mmh.com/images/site/MMH1207_SpRpt_Top20Software.pdf.

Gartner Consulting Services Overview. http://www.gartner.com/technology/consulting/.

Gartner. *Magic Quadrants.* http://www.gartner.com/technology/research/methodologies/research_mq.jsp.

Gartner: Office of the Ombudsman. http://www.gartner.com/imagesrv/research/methodologies/oo_brochure.pdf.

Gartner Research Methodologies. http://www.gartner.com/technology/research/methodologies/methodology.jsp.

Gartner Says Worldwide Supply Chain Management Software Market Grew 12.3 Percent to Reach $7.7 Billion in 2011. Last modified May 16, 2012. http://www.gartner.com/newsroom/id/2016915.

Hollander, Nathan. *A Guide to Software Package Evaluation and Selection: The R2ISC Method.* AMACOM, 2000.

Hammond, Tina. May 1, 2013. *Research: 76% of IT leaders satisfied with enterprise software.* http://www.zdnet.com/research-76-of-it-leaders-satisfied-with-enterprise-software-7000014665/.

Harris, Derrick. *Gartner Gets It Wrong with Cloud Quadrant.* January 4, 2011. http://gigaom.com/2011/01/04/gartner-gets-it-wrong-with-cloud-quadrant/.

Howcroft, Debra and Light, Ben. *A Study of User Involvement in Packaged Software Selection.* University of Salford: 2002. http://scholar.googleusercontent.com/scholar?q=cache:JnAMHhyBPyAJ:scholar.google.com/+software+selection&hl=en&as_sdt=0,5.

Howlett, Dennis. *Gartner in the dock over Magic Quadrant.* October 20, 2009. http://www.zdnet.com/blog/howlett/gartner-in-the-dock-over-magic-quadrant/1424.

Krugman, Paul. Berating the Raters. *New York Times*: April 25, 2010. http://www.nytimes.com/2010/04/26/opinion/26krugman.html?_r=0.

Leonhard, Woody. *Gartner and IDC predictions: Oops, forget what we said last time.* InfoWorld: April 4, 2013. http://www.infoworld.com/t/microsoft-windows/gartner-and-idc-predictions-oops-forget-what-we-said-last-time-215830.

Magic Quadrant. Last modified July 8, 2013. http://en.wikipedia.org/wiki/Magic_Quadrant.

Mendel, Gregor. Last modified June 7, 2013. http://en.wikipedia.org/wiki/Gregor_Mendel.

Mendel, Gregor: A Private Scientist.
   http://www.nature.com/scitable/topicpage/gregor-mendel-a-private-scientist-
   6618227.

Mendel, Gregor. *Experiments in Plant Hybridization.* 1865.
   http://www.mendelweb.org/Mendel.html.

Network Effect. Last modified July 4, 2013. http://en.wikipedia.org/wiki/
   Network_effect.

Obal, Philip. *Selecting Warehouse Software from WMS & ERP Providers, Expanded
   Edition: Find the Best Warehouse Module or Warehouse Management System.*
   Industrial Data & Information Inc., 2007.

Pelz-Sharpe, Alan. *De-mystifying the Gartner ECM Magic Quadrant.* September 28,
   2007. http://www.realstorygroup.com/Blog/1023-De-mystifying-the-Gartner-ECM-
   Magic-Quadrant.

Reames, Patrick and Vasey, Dr. Gary M. *Selecting and Implementing Energy Trading,
   Transaction and Risk Management Software: A Primer.* BookSurge, 2008.

Reuter, Jonathan and Zitzewitz, Eric. *Do ads influence editors?
   Advertising and bias in the financial media.* Draft: August 2005. https://docs
   .google.com/viewer?url=https%3A%2F%2Fwww2.bc.edu%2Fjonathan-reuter%
   2Fresearch%2Fads.pdf.

Schaeffer, Chuck. *Truths When Selecting Supply Chain Management Software.*
   http://www.allsupplychain.com/supply-chain-software-fit.php.

Scientific Method. Last modified June 11, 2013. https://en.wikipedia.org/wiki/
   Scientific_method.

Standards for High-Quality Research and Analysis.
   http://www.rand.org/standards.html.

Snapp, Shaun. *The Real Story Behind ERP: Separating Fact from Fiction.* SCM
   Focus Press, 2013

Whitehorn, Mark. Is Gartner's Magic Quadrant really magic? *The Register:* March
   31, 2007. http://www.theregister.co.uk/2007/03/31/myth_gartner_magic_quadrant/.
   http://grc2020.com/blog/rethinking-grc-analyst-rant-gartners-2012-egrc-magic-
   quadrant/

Author Profile

Shaun Snapp is the Founder and Editor of SCM Focus. SCM Focus is one of the largest independent supply chain software analysis and educational sites on the Internet.

After working at several of the largest consulting companies and at i2 Technologies, he became an independent consultant and later started SCM Focus. He maintains a strong interest in comparative software design, and works both in SAP APO, as well as with a variety of best-of-breed supply chain planning vendors. His ongoing relationships with these vendors keep him on the cutting edge of emerging technology.

Primary Sources of Information and Writing Topics

Shaun writes about topics with which he has first-hand experience. These topics range from recovering problematic implementations, to system configuration, to socializing complex software and supply chain concepts in the areas of demand planning, supply planning and production planning.

More broadly, he writes on topics supportive of these applications, which include master data parameter management, integration, analytics, simulation and bill of material management systems. He covers management aspects of enterprise software ranging from software policy to handling consulting partners on SAP projects.

Shaun writes from an implementer's perspective and as a result he focuses on how software is actually used in practice rather than its hypothetical or "pure release note capabilities." Unlike many authors in enterprise software who keep their distance from discussing the realities of software implementation, he writes both on the problems as well as the successes of his software use. This gives him a distinctive voice in the field.

Secondary Sources of Information

In addition to project experience, Shaun's interest in academic literature is a secondary source of information for his books and articles. Intrigued with the historical perspective of supply chain software, much of his writing is influenced by his readings and research into how different categories of supply chain software developed, evolved, and finally became broadly used over time.

Covering the Latest Software Developments

Shaun is focused on supply chain software selections and implementation improvement through writing and consulting, bringing companies some of the newest technologies and methods. Some of the software developments that Shaun showcases at SCM Focus and in books at SCM Focus Press have yet to reach widespread adoption.

Education

Shaun has an undergraduate degree in business from the University of Hawaii, a Masters of Science in Maritime Management from the Maine Maritime Academy and a Masters of Science in Business Logistics from Penn State University. He has taught both logistics and SAP software.

Software Certifications
Shaun has been trained and/or certified in products from i2 Technologies, Servigistics, ToolsGroup and SAP (SD, DP, SNP, SPP, EWM).

Contact
Shaun can be contacted at: shaunsnapp@scmfocus.com

Abbreviations

ERP—Enterprise Resource Planning

RFP—Request for Proposal

SaaS—Software as a Service

SAP BW—Business Warehouse

SAP PI—SAP Process Integration

TCO—Total Cost of Ownership

www.ingramcontent.com/pod-product-compliance
Lightning Source LLC
La Vergne TN
LVHW080100070326
832902LV00014B/2336